# Meatless Cooking

# Meatless Cooking

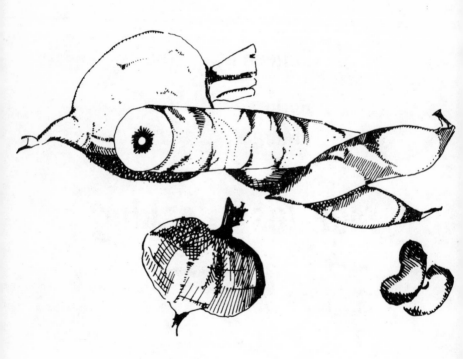

# Pegeen's
## vegetarian recipes

by
**Pegeen Fitzgerald**

Recipes arranged by
**Margaret Smith**

GRAMERCY PUBLISHING COMPANY • NEW YORK

**MEATLESS COOKING: Pegeen's Vegetarian Recipes**
**by Pegeen Fitzgerald, arranged by Margaret Smith**

© MCMLXVIII by Pegeen Fitzgerald

Library of Congress Catalog Card Number: 68-13647

This edition published by Gramercy Publishing Company
a division of Crown Publishers, Inc.,
by arrangement with Prentice-Hall, Inc.

b    c    d    e    f    g    h

Printed in the United States of America

# FOREWORD

As you know, I am a vegetarian. My belief comes not only from an innate reverence for life but from a love of animals. As most of our listeners know, our New York City apartment and our log cabin in the woods are both miniature zoos. Homeless strays seem to find us and we in turn shelter as many as possible and try to find good homes for the others.

It was a visit to a slaughterhouse that made a fervent vegetarian out of me. The experience was so soul-shattering that I could never again touch meat, fowl or fish. Yet I find myself healthy and well nourished.

How could I have been a "humanitarian" for so many, many years without once having a sobering thought about the ethics of eating animals!

It must have been mindlessness, purely and simply; the moment I decided never again to eat flesh, fowl or fish . . . a great contentment took over my heart and I finally knew peace of mind.

True, it is a militant kind of peace . . . for ethical vegetarians are constantly called upon to defend their stand. And the fact that neither friend nor stranger seems able to sit at table with one who eats nothing that has ever been alive without insisting on knowing "why" she abstains . . . well, that constant questioning makes for daily proselytizing.

And I do it eagerly!

If not queried, would I myself bring the subject up?

Probably.

But it is never necessary! And this longing to know why some of us prefer loving animals to eating them indicates to me that a constant yearning for true kinship with all that lives and breathes is common to us all.

The promises to the spirit and the body are as eternal as the appearance of spring. The vegetarian's diet is really a matter of the heart and of belief. And among the great men who because of their reverence for life avoided meat as an article of diet are these: Socrates, Plato, St. Francis of Assisi, Leonardo da Vinci, Sir Isaac Newton, William Blake, Paganini, Henry D. Thoreau, Horace Greeley, George Bernard Shaw, Albert Einstein, Mahatma Gandhi, and Albert Schweitzer.

Someday I will write a book about vegans and vegetarians . . . with no recipes at all . . . and it will be about man's longing to be truly kind.

# INTRODUCTION

This collection of recipes—some of them my own, others from friends, and a great percentage from generous listeners to our program—is offered to the cook who happens to like serving vegetables as well as to the man or woman who has made vegetarianism a philosophy of life.

The process of relying solely on vegetables, fruits and grains has naturally tested my imagination. I do not, incidentally, eat eggs myself, although I serve them to my guests and have included them in this book. Canned soups are featured, too, because they are so often used by other cooks in a variety of dishes and are short cuts when one must cook in a hurry.

Herbs and condiments are important in vegetarian cooking, and it is suggested that the cook use his or her imagination and experiment. Most of the recipes included are simply made and are wonderfully good for your health.

The vegetarian doesn't eat by the seasons; he is probably less dependent on them than the meat-eater. The vegetarian has no meals built around spring lamb or Thanksgiving turkey or Christmas goose. Nuts are a year-round source of protein, and you'll find that you often build a meal around rice, potatoes, wheat or spaghetti.

Those who love mushrooms will have them fresh or canned or dried at every opportunity.

No longer is there a label "out of season" on most vegetables a good part of the year. The winter fare of our grandfathers—cabbages, turnips, pumpkins stored in the cold cellar—has been enlarged by the miracle of transportation, refrigeration and quick freezing. Fresh vegetables and fruits in the winter months, when the body craves them, are now possible. What is more invigorating, what promises more richly the springtime than a salad of new greens, or fresh peas with mint or a crisp tangy apple and coleslaw salad?

The concise and simple step-by-step directions in this book should appeal, hopefully, to the beginner, the bride, as well as to the more experienced cook, who is limited nevertheless by time or a career. These recipes have been developed with measurements that can easily be reduced or multiplied by very simple arithmetic, unless noted.

The image of a vegetable plate as served in most restaurants may be a deterrent to many cooks when they first think of serving mainly menus of vegetables and fruits. But vegetables prepared at home are quite different, and two vegetables, a good whole wheat bread and fruit can make a healthy, satisfying, and vitamin-rich meal.

# CONTENTS

# NOTES FOR YOUR HELP

These recipes have been developed with measurements that can easily be reduced or multiplied by very simple arithmetic, unless noted.

In making smaller amounts, allow less time for baking, etc. In preparing larger amounts, allow more time.

Sometimes the time given for baking will differ according to the size of the baking dish used. If a glass baking dish is used, lower the oven temperature 25 degrees.

It is difficult to say how many servings a recipe will make as appetites differ. Needless to say, sometimes the dish will be the main item at the meal; at other times, a side dish. So, use your own discretion as to the number of servings you wish.

When selecting eggplants, choose one with an elongated blossom scar. It will have fewer seeds than one with a round blossom scar.

If you wish to use fresh parsley instead of dried, double the amount specified in the recipe.

If fresh tomatoes are in season, they may be substituted for canned tomatoes provided they are peeled and chopped.

Roux is the French name for the blended mixture of flour and fat used to thicken sauces.

MSG is the abbreviation for monosodium glutamate.

To scald milk, heat over simmering water until a thin film forms on top, or bubbles appear around the edges.

If an uneven number of eggs is required in a recipe and you wish to reduce it, use a whole egg rather than a half, unless noted on the recipe.

A soufflé will rise better if you butter only the bottom of your baking dish. Ever try to climb a greased pole? Egg whites have the same trouble!

A wire whisk is much more satisfactory than a spoon for sauce making.

A vegetarian diet is the acid test of humanitarianism.

Tolstoy

# Meatless Cooking

# Vegetables

"May I venture to express an opinion on the large amount of space and attention given to the subject of humane slaughter? May not all this agitation act as a red herring drawn across the road to the ABOLITION of slaughter of animals for food in every shape and form? The suffering caused by the death blow or stab, even though it may be a matter of minutes, is nothing compared to the suffering of transport—the driving from meadows to a station, forcing by tail-twisting, etc., into trucks or the holds of vessels, the smell of blood at the yards, a crescendo of moral fear overpowered by the greater cruelty of the drovers. MAY NOT HUMANE SLAUGHTER ACT AS A CONSCIENCE-SOOTHER FOR MEAT-EATERS? Some day—it may be fifty or it may be a thousand years hence—meat eating will be regarded as a relic of savagery (for compassion is slowly but surely winning its way into the hearts of mankind) and, therefore, it should not be regarded as a hopeless task to hasten that day. Slavery was not stopped in British lands by concentrating on some one phase of its cruelty. Moreover its abolition might have been long delayed by amelioration of its most obvious forms of cruelty. Eating animals is damnable from numerous points of view, and as bad or worse for the human race as it is for the animals driven to the slaughterhouse."

W. B. Pease from "Progress Today"

# ASPARAGUS–MUSHROOM BAKE

     2 cups day-old bread crumbs
    ¼ cup melted butter or margarine
    ½ cup homogenized milk
    ½ cup cream
     1 8-ounce can sliced mushrooms or
        ½ pound fresh mushrooms
     1 pound cooked cut asparagus spears,
        drained
       Salt and pepper
     2 teaspoons instant onion flakes

1. Use firm-style bread. Toss crumbs in melted butter or margarine. Place half in a buttered casserole.

2. Combine milk and cream and pour half over the crumbs.

3. If fresh mushrooms are used, sauté briefly in 1 tablespoon butter or margarine. Place mushrooms on bread crumbs, and the asparagus over the mushrooms. Lightly sprinkle with salt and pepper and sprinkle onion flakes on top.

4. Sprinkle remaining crumbs on top; pour remaining milk over crumbs.

5. Bake about 25 minutes in a 375° oven.

# BAKED ASPARAGUS CUSTARD

2 cups cooked cut asparagus spears,
    drained
1⅓ cups milk, scalded
4 eggs, well beaten
1 teaspoon salt
    Dash of pepper

1. Place asparagus pieces in a well-buttered baking dish.
2. Add scalded milk to eggs; add seasonings. Pour over asparagus.
3. Set baking dish in pan of hot water and bake in a 350° oven 30 minutes or until a knife inserted in the middle comes out clean.

*Note: This may be cooked in a double boiler over low heat. It would take less time.*

# ASPARAGUS-FILLED CRÊPES

2 crêpes
2 large stalks cooked asparagus
    Mornay sauce, mushroom sauce or
      Cheddar cheese sauce

1. Roll crêpe around asparagus.
2. Put two crêpes in individual serving dish or oven-proof platter. Pour sauce over.
3. Place in hot oven 400° for about 10 minutes. Serves 1.

# BARLEY PILAF

1 cup chopped onion
1 cup chopped celery
2 tablespoons butter
1 cup barley
4 cups boiling water
1 teaspoon salt

1. Sauté onion and celery in butter in a heavy skillet. Add barley and brown.
2. Add boiling water and salt.
3. Cook over low heat until water is absorbed and barley is tender, about 1 hour.

# WEST VIRGINIA GREEN BEANS

1 medium onion, chopped
1 tablespoon oil
1 tablespoon flour
¾ cup liquid from beans
1 tablespoon vinegar
¼ teaspoon celery seed
  Salt and pepper to taste
2 cups cooked green beans

1. Brown onion in the oil. Add the flour and stir until brown.

2. Add reserved liquid from beans and the vinegar and celery seed. Season with salt and pepper.

3. Add beans and heat together.

*Note: Leftovers may be served as a salad.*

# GREEN BEANS WITH MUSHROOMS

1 small can mushrooms
¼ cup mushroom liquid
1 pound green beans, cut in 1-inch
    pieces
2 tablespoons peanut oil
1 small onion, cut fine
2 teaspoons salt
¼ teaspoon sugar
¼ cup cream

1. Drain mushrooms, reserving ¼ cup of the liquid.
2. Put mushrooms with beans in a heavy pot and add oil, onion, mushroom liquid, salt and sugar. Turn heat low and cook until tender.
3. Add cream, heat well and serve.

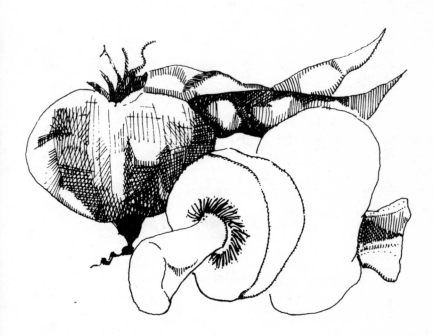

# GREEN BEANS WITH HERBS

1 pound green beans, cut in 1-inch
    pieces
2 tablespoons peanut oil
1 tablespoon instant chopped onion
    Dash of garlic powder
½ teaspoon basil
½ teaspoon rosemary
    Salt to taste
¼ cup water

1. Put all ingredients in a heavy saucepan or electric skillet.
2. Cover and cook until tender-crisp.

# GREEN BEANS PARMESAN

½ cup chopped onion
2 tablespoons butter
2 cups cooked green beans
    Salt and pepper
2 tablespoons grated Parmesan cheese

1. Sauté onion in butter until lightly browned.
2. Toss onion with hot green beans; add salt and pepper to taste.
3. Put in serving dish and sprinkle cheese over top of beans.

"Vegetable eaters—especially if they avoid condiments as well as flesh and fish—are not apt to be thirsty."

Wm. A. Alcott, M.D.

## PAN-FRIED GREEN BEANS

2 tablespoons peanut oil
1 pound green beans, cut in 1-inch
    pieces
1 teaspoon salt
    Dash of MSG
¼ cup water
2 tablespoons slivered almonds

1. Heat electric skillet to 350°. Add oil and beans, salt and MSG. Stir well and add the water.

2. Cover skillet and cook until tender-crisp, about 10 minutes. Garnish with almonds.

# BAKED KIDNEY BEANS AND COTTAGE CHEESE

1 teaspoon instant onion flakes
1 teaspoon dried parsley flakes
1 tablespoon pickle relish
  Salt
2 tablespoons catsup
1 cup cottage cheese
2 cups cooked kidney beans, drained
1 cup buttered bread crumbs

1. Combine onion flakes, parsley, pickle relish, salt, catsup and cottage cheese. Add to beans, mixing lightly.

2. Pour into buttered baking dish. Sprinkle crumbs on top.

3. Place in 375° oven and bake until crumbs are brown and beans are heated through.

# BAKED LIMA BEANS AND PEANUTS

1 cup mashed potatoes
1¼ cups cooked lima beans, drained
½ cup roasted, shelled peanuts,
    chopped fine
1 egg, slightly beaten
⅓ cup milk
½ teaspoon salt
    Dash of pepper, paprika
1 teaspoon grated onion

1. Put half the potatoes in a buttered baking dish, add half the beans, then half the peanuts. Repeat.

2. Combine egg, milk, seasonings and onion. Pour over the other ingredients. Bake in a hot oven 375° about 25 minutes.

3. Serve with cheese or tomato sauce.

# ESCALLOPED LIMA BEANS AND CABBAGE

2 cups cooked shredded cabbage
2 cups cooked fresh or frozen lima
    beans
1 can condensed cream of celery soup
½ cup grated Cheddar cheese
1 tablespoon very fine dry bread
    crumbs

1. Combine cabbage, lima beans, soup and cheese. Pour into greased casserole. Sprinkle crumbs over top.
2. Bake in 375° oven just long enough to heat through.

# BAKED LIMA BEANS

2 cups cooked dried lima beans
¼ cup catsup
¼ cup tomato sauce
1 teaspoon instant onion flakes
1 teaspoon chili powder
1 teaspoon prepared mustard
1 tablespoon brown sugar

1. Drain beans.
2. Combine remaining ingredients. Add beans and pour into a baking dish.
3. Bake in a 375° oven until heated through.

# CURRIED LIMA BEANS

½ teaspoon curry powder
½ teaspoon salt
½ cup heavy cream
2 cups cooked lima beans

1. Mix salt and curry powder with cream.
2. Add lima beans and heat until well seasoned. Serve very hot.

*Note: More or less curry powder may be used, according to your taste.*

# BAKED LIMA BEANS AND MUSHROOMS

¼ cup chopped onion
2 tablespoons butter or margarine
1 cup sliced fresh mushrooms or
    1 small can, drained
1 can condensed mushroom soup
½ cup milk or mushroom liquid from
    canned mushrooms
2 cups cooked, drained lima beans

1. Sauté onion in butter or margarine until golden. If fresh mushrooms are used, add and sauté them a few minutes.

2. Combine soup with milk or reserved mushroom liquid. Add onions and mushrooms.

3. Add beans to soup mixture, stirring lightly. Pour into buttered baking dish.

4. Bake in a 350° oven until hot and bubbly.

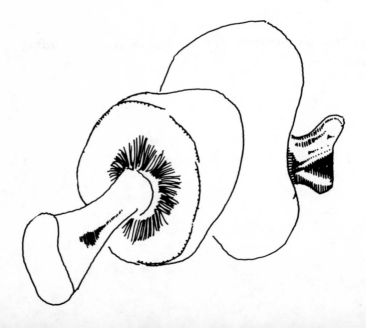

# DELUXE LIMAS

3 cups cooked lima beans
¼ cup tomato sauce
1 can condensed mushroom soup
¼ teaspoon basil
1 tablespoon white wine (optional)

1. Cook limas. Drain.
2. Heat tomato sauce and soup with the basil. Add to limas and simmer a few minutes to combine flavors. Add wine and serve.

# CHEESE–BEAN PATTIES

1 cup grated American cheese
1½ cups cooked dried beans
1½ cups mashed potatoes
    Salt and pepper to taste
2 tablespoons grated onion
½ teaspoon MSG

1. Combine all ingredients; taste for seasoning.
2. Shape into patties ½-inch thick. Dip into flour or cornmeal.
3. Sauté on both sides until brown in hot oil.
4. Serve with tomato, cheese or horseradish sauce.

*Note: Any kind of dried beans or dried peas may be used.*

# THREE-BEAN COMBO

1-pound can vegetarian baked beans
1-pound can red kidney beans
1-pound can cooked soaked dried lima
    beans
¼ cup molasses
1 tablespoon instant onion
2 teaspoons dry mustard
¼ cup catsup

1. Drain lima beans and red kidney beans.
2. Combine all ingredients. Pour into a casserole and bake until heated through.

# BEETS WITH PINEAPPLE

2 tablespoons brown sugar
1 tablespoon cornstarch
¼ teaspoon salt
1 small can crushed pineapple
1 tablespoon cider vinegar
1 tablespoon butter or margarine
2 cups sliced cooked beets, drained

1. Combine sugar, cornstarch and salt in saucepan.
2. Add crushed pineapple and vinegar and cook until it thickens, stirring constantly. Add butter or margarine and beets. Simmer a few minutes longer to heat and season well.

## BEETS IN CITRUS SAUCE

    1 one-pound can beets, drained
      Liquid from beets
      Juice and rind of ½ lemon
    1 tablespoon frozen orange juice
        concentrate
    1 tablespoon cornstarch
    2 tablespoons sugar
      Dash of cloves
    ½ teaspoon salt
    1 tablespoon margarine or butter


1. Combine the beet juice, lemon juice and rind and the orange concentrate.

2. Mix the cornstarch, sugar, cloves and salt. Add to the beet juice, beating with a wire whisk. Cook until clear.

3. Add the beets and butter to the sauce. Heat until the flavors are well blended.

# BROCCOLI–CHEESE CUSTARD

2 cups partially cooked chopped
    broccoli
Salt and pepper
1½ cups grated sharp Cheddar cheese
1½ cups milk, scalded
1 tablespoon minced onion
3 eggs, slightly beaten

1. Cook broccoli until it loses its bright green color.
Drain.
2. Put half the broccoli in a casserole, sprinkle with
salt and pepper and half the cheese. Repeat.
3. Add milk and onion to eggs; pour over broccoli.
4. Set in pan of hot water and bake in a 350° oven
until firm in the middle, about 40 minutes.

# BRUSSELS SPROUTS WITH
# GREEN GRAPES

1 box frozen Brussels sprouts
2 tablespoons butter or margarine
¼ cup slivered almonds
½ cup seedless green grapes

1. Cook sprouts until tender. Drain.
2. Melt butter; add almonds and stir until lightly
browned.
3. Add the seedless grapes, splitting them if large, and
heat a few minutes longer.
4. Mix the almonds and grapes with the sprouts carefully.

# BRUSSELS SPROUTS WITH CITRUS SAUCE

1 10-ounce box frozen Brussels sprouts
2 tablespoons butter or margarine
2 tablespoons flour
1 cup milk, scalded
1 egg yolk, slightly beaten
1 tablespoon frozen orange concentrate
1 tablespoon lemon juice

1. Cook Brussels sprouts. Drain.

2. Make a roux of the butter and flour. Whip into milk and stir until it thickens.

3. Add some of the sauce to egg yolk, mix and return to sauce. Cook a little longer. Add orange and lemon juice, stirring constantly. Pour over sprouts.

# SERBIAN CABBAGE

½ medium cabbage, coarsely shredded
1 green pepper, cut in rings
1 onion, cut in rings
1 teaspoon salt
2 tablespoons peanut oil
1 large tomato, diced

1. Heat electric skillet to 350°. Add oil.
2. Add vegetables and salt. Stir well and cover.
3. Cook until tender-crisp, about 10 minutes.

# RED CABBAGE, GERMAN STYLE

4 cups shredded raw red cabbage
½ cup boiling water
1 sour apple, peeled and chopped
1 small onion
6 cloves
2 tablespoons butter
2 tablespoons brown sugar
½ teaspoon salt
2 tablespoons vinegar

1. Add cabbage to boiling water with apple, and the cloves stuck into the onion. Cover and cook until tender.
2. Remove onion and cloves.
3. Add butter, sugar, salt and vinegar just before serving.

# FRANK'S CABBAGE AND NOODLES

    3 tablespoons butter or margarine
    3 cups coarsely shredded cabbage
    ¼ pound medium egg noodles
      Salt and pepper

1. Melt butter or margarine in heavy skillet or electric skillet set at 350°. Add cabbage and stir frequently until golden brown.

2. Cook noodles. Drain and rinse with boiling water. Add to cabbage. Season to taste with salt and pepper.

3. Let mixture stand over low heat a few minutes to season and serve hot.

## PAN-FRIED CABBAGE

4 tablespoons butter
1 medium cabbage, shredded
Salt and pepper to taste

1. Melt butter in heavy skillet or electric frypan.
2. Add cabbage, salt and pepper. Cover tightly and cook about 10 minutes, stirring occasionally.

## CURRIED CABBAGE

4 cups shredded cabbage
1 cooking apple, peeled and diced
2 teaspoons instant onion flakes
½ cup sour cream
1 teaspoon curry powder
Salt to taste

1. Cook cabbage with apple and onion in a small amount of water until barely tender. Drain.

2. Add sour cream, curry powder and salt to cabbage. Reheat over low heat.

## HOT SLAW WITH PINEAPPLE

    3 cups shredded cabbage
    ¼ cup crushed pineapple
    2 tablespoons vinegar
    1 egg, slightly beaten
    ¼ teaspoon dry mustard
    ½ teaspoon salt

1. Cook cabbage till tender-crisp. Drain.

2. Combine remaining ingredients in top of double boiler and stir constantly until thick.

3. Add cabbage to sauce and heat until flavors are well blended.

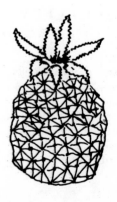

# CARROTS WITH PINEAPPLE

1 bunch carrots (one pound)
2 tablespoons chopped onion
2 tablespoons butter or margarine
4 slices pineapple, drained and cut
      in pieces
¼ teaspoon dried dill weed
   Salt and pepper to taste
1 teaspoon sugar

1. Slice carrots and boil in salted water until tender-crisp. Drain.

2. Sauté onion in butter until golden. Combine with pineapple and dill. Stir until heated through.

3. Combine pineapple mixture and carrots. Season with sugar, salt and pepper.

# CARROTS AND CELERY ALMONDINE

1 bunch carrots
2 cups celery, sliced crosswise in ¼-inch
      pieces
2 tablespoons butter or margarine
4 tablespoons slivered almonds
2 teaspoons sugar
2 tablespoons lemon juice
   Salt to taste

1. Cook carrots and celery separately in a small amount of boiling salted water until barely tender. Drain.

2. Meanwhile, heat butter or margarine; add almonds and sugar and stir over low heat until nuts have browned.

3. Add nuts and lemon juice to vegetables; mix lightly and salt to taste.

# CARROT–WALNUT PATTIES

1 pound carrots
2 eggs
2 tablespoons flour
½ teaspoon salt
½ teaspoon sugar
⅛ teaspoon pepper
¼ cup chopped walnuts

1. Cook carrots; drain.
2. Put all ingredients, except nuts, into the blender. Blend until well mixed. Add walnuts.
3. Heat electric skillet to 375°.
4. Fry by spoonfuls in oil until brown. Turn and brown other side.

# SWEET-SOUR CARROTS

⅓ cup vinegar
½ cup sugar
½ teaspoon salt
2 tablespoons butter
4 cups cooked, sliced carrots

1. Heat vinegar; add sugar, salt and butter; stirring until the sugar dissolves and the butter melts.
2. Put carrots in a casserole. Pour the vinegar mixture over and bake in a 350° oven about 25 minutes.

# GLAZED CARROTS AND ONIONS

    1 bunch carrots
    1 buffet can boiled onions, drained
    2 tablespoons butter or margarine
    4 tablespoons white corn syrup
    2 tablespoons light brown sugar
    1 tablespoon lemon juice
    ¼ teaspoon salt
    2 tablespoons sliced, toasted almonds
    1 tablespoon chopped parsley


1. Cut carrots into fairly large pieces. Cook and drain.
2. Put drained onions and carrots into a shallow baking dish.
3. Combine butter or margarine with corn syrup, brown sugar, lemon juice and salt. Bring to a boil.
4. Pour syrup over vegetables and place in a 400° oven 15 minutes, until well glazed, turning once.
5. Serve hot with almonds and parsley as a garnish.


*Note: If you like, simmer the vegetables in the glaze in a saucepan over low heat instead of heating in the oven.*

# HONEY-GLAZED CARROTS

1 bunch carrots, cut in 2-inch lengths
2 tablespoons butter
¼ cup honey

1. Cook carrots in salted water until barely tender. If very large, cut in half lengthwise before cutting in 2-inch pieces. Drain.
2. Melt butter, add honey and bring to a boil. Add carrots, turning frequently until well glazed.

# GERMAN CARROTS

1 pound carrots, sliced
1 tablespoon butter
1 tablespoon flour
¾ cup carrot liquid
Dash of pepper
Few gratings of nutmeg
½ teaspoon sugar

1. Cook carrots in salted water until tender. Drain, reserving ¾ cup of the liquid.
2. Melt butter, stir in flour to form a roux. Add reserved liquid from the carrots, pepper, nutmeg and sugar. Bring to a boil and add the carrots.
3. Let stand a few minutes to season through.

# MASHED CARROTS WITH SOUR CREAM

    1 bunch carrots
    Salt
    Generous dash of pepper
    ½ teaspoon dried parsley flakes
    ¼ cup sour cream

1. Cook carrots until tender in boiling salted water. Drain.

2. Mash carrots. Add pepper, parsley flakes and sour cream. Serve very hot.

# CARROT RAISIN PUFF

2 cups grated raw carrots
2 tablespoons butter
2 tablespoons flour
1 teaspoon sugar
1 teaspoon salt
½ teaspoon curry powder
1 cup milk
½ cup grated American cheese
¼ cup raisins
2 eggs, separated

1. Scald milk in double boiler. Melt butter, blend in flour, sugar, salt and curry powder. Whip into milk, beating until thick and smooth. Add cheese, stirring until it melts. Add raisins and carrots.

2. Beat egg yolks, add some of the sauce; blend and return to double boiler. Cook a few minutes longer.

3. Beat egg whites until stiff but not dry and fold into mixture.

4. Pour into a baking dish, the bottom buttered, and bake at 325° for about 45 minutes or until firm.

## MARMALADE-GLAZED CARROTS

1 bunch carrots, cut in rather large
   pieces
2 tablespoons butter
¼ cup marmalade
¼ teaspoon ginger

1. Cook carrots in salted water until barely tender. Drain.

2. Melt butter, add marmalade and ginger. Bring to a boil. Add carrots and keep turning until well glazed.

## CAULIFLOWER DELISH

1 medium cauliflower, cut in pieces
1 can condensed cream of celery soup
½ cup grated Swiss cheese
½ cup milk or cream

1. Cook cauliflower until barely tender.
2. Heat soup in double boiler. Add grated cheese and milk. Serve over cauliflower.
3. If desired, put cauliflower and sauce in a casserole, top with buttered crumbs and heat in the oven long enough to brown crumbs.

# CAULIFLOWER WITH SOUR CREAM

1 medium cauliflower
1 cup sour cream
½ teaspoon dried dill weed
2 tablespoons lemon juice
½ teaspoon salt

1. Separate cauliflower into medium pieces. Cook until barely tender. Drain.
2. Combine sour cream with remaining ingredients.
3. Put cauliflower in a baking dish and pour sour cream mixture over. Place in 350° oven long enough to heat through.

# DEEP-FRIED CAULIFLOWER

1 small cauliflower
1 cup pancake mix
1 cup tomato sauce
  Fine dry bread crumbs

1. Wash cauliflower. Cut into uniform flowerets. Cook until almost done. Drain.
2. Dredge cauliflower in pancake mix.
3. Dip flowerets in tomato sauce, drain and roll in bread crumbs. Let set 15 minutes.
4. Fry in deep hot fat, 375° until brown.

*Note: Other vegetables may be prepared this way—strips of raw eggplant, cooked carrots, etc.*

# CAULIFLOWER AND MUSHROOMS

 1 medium head cauliflower, broken into
    flowerets
 2 tablespoons butter or margarine
 ½ pound fresh mushrooms, sliced
 ¼ cup chopped green pepper
 2 tablespoons chopped onion
 ¼ cup chopped pimiento
 1 can condensed Cheddar cheese soup

1. Cook cauliflower until barely tender in boiling salted water. Drain.

2. Sauté mushrooms, green pepper and onion in butter or margarine for 5 minutes.

3. Add sautéed vegetables and pimiento to soup.

4. Put cauliflower in a buttered baking dish and pour soup mixture over it. Heat in a 375° oven until very hot.

# POLKA DOT CELERY

3 cups celery, cut in ¼-inch pieces
1 tablespoon butter
2 tablespoons flour
½ cup celery stock
½ cup milk
1 tablespoon minced green pepper
1 tablespoon minced onion
2 teaspoons pimiento, cut in pieces
⅛ cup grated sharp American cheese
Salt and pepper to taste

1. Cook celery until tender-crisp. Drain, reserving ½ cup of the stock.
2. Melt butter, add flour to form a roux. Add milk and celery stock. Bring to a boil. Add pepper, onion, pimiento and cheese, stirring well to blend. Cook until thick.
3. Add celery and serve.

# CORN PUDDING

1-pound can cream-style corn
2 eggs, slightly beaten
1 teaspoon sugar
1 tablespoon melted butter
1 teaspoon salt
Dash of pepper
2 cups milk, scalded

1. Combine the corn with the eggs and seasonings.
2. Add milk slowly. Pour into a buttered baking dish.
3. Set the baking dish in a pan of hot water and bake in a 350° oven until a knife inserted in the middle comes out clean.

# CHEESED CORN AND GREEN BEANS

2 cups cooked whole-kernel corn,
   drained
2 cups cooked green beans, drained
2 tablespoons chopped pimiento
1 can condensed Cheddar cheese soup
   Crushed sesame crackers

1. Combine corn, beans, pimiento and soup. Pour into a greased baking dish.

2. Top with crushed crackers and heat in a 375° oven until brown and bubbly.

# CORN RAREBIT

1 can condensed cream of celery soup
¼ cup finely chopped green pepper
¼ cup finely chopped onion
2 tablespoons chopped pimiento
½ pound shredded Cheddar cheese
2 cups corn

1. Heat soup with pepper, onion, pimiento and cheese in double boiler until cheese is melted.

2. Add corn and continue cooking over low heat until very hot.

3. Serve on toast.

# "RAINED-OUT" CORN ROAST

1. Husk corn, removing all silk.
2. Brush with melted butter and sprinkle with salt and pepper. If desired, add a few instant onion flakes.
3. Wrap corn in foil, sealing well.
4. Bake in 375° oven for 15 minutes.

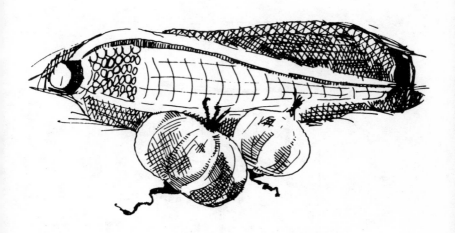

# CORN AND EGG SCRAMBLE

1 tablespoon butter
1 cup cooked whole-kernel corn
1 medium tomato, peeled
4 eggs, slightly beaten
  Salt and pepper to taste

1. Melt butter in heavy skillet; add corn and tomatoes and heat.

2. Add eggs, salt and pepper, and cook over low heat until eggs are set, stirring constantly.

# ESCALLOPED CORN AND TOMATOES

1-pound can tomatoes, broken up
1-pound can whole-kernel corn, drained
½ teaspoon instant onion flakes
6 slices buttered bread
    Salt and pepper to taste

1. Combine tomatoes, corn, onion flakes. Salt and pepper to taste.
2. Put a third of the vegetables in a buttered baking dish. Cover with two slices of the bread, cutting to fit the dish. Repeat.
3. Put remaining third of vegetables over the bread. Cut remaining two slices of bread into cubes and sprinkle over top of vegetables. Heat in a 350° oven until brown and bubbly.

# SAUTÉED CORN

1 ear of corn
1 tablespoon chopped onion
2 teaspoons butter
    Salt and pepper

1. Melt butter in heavy skillet; add onion and pepper.
2. Cut corn from cob and add to skillet.
3. Cook five minutes, stirring frequently.

# EGGPLANT EN CASSEROLE

       1 egg
       2 tablespoons water
       1 medium eggplant, peeled and sliced
           in 1-inch slices
         Oil for sautéing
    1½ cups tomato puree
       ½ teaspoon basil
       ½ teaspoon oregano
       1 teaspoon salt
       ⅛ teaspoon garlic powder
       ½ pound mozzarella cheese, grated


1. Beat egg and water. Dip eggplant in mixture and sauté quickly in hot oil until brown. Set aside.

2. Mix puree with basil, oregano, salt and garlic powder.

3. In a greased casserole make layers of eggplant, tomato puree and cheese.

4. Bake in a 375° oven about 35 minutes until brown and bubbly.

# SAUTÉED EGGPLANT PARMESAN

1 medium eggplant
½ cup buttermilk
½ cup dry bread crumbs
Dash of garlic salt
¼ teaspoon oregano
2 tablespoons grated Parmesan cheese
½ teaspoon salt
Vegetable oil

1. Peel eggplant and slice in 1-inch slices.

2. Dip slices in buttermilk, then in crumbs, which have been mixed with garlic salt, oregano, salt, and grated cheese.

3. Sauté in oil in a heavy skillet, turning to brown each side.

# EGGPLANT SAUTÉ

1 egg, slightly beaten
⅓ cup milk
½ teaspoon salt
Pepper to taste
Eggplant, cut in ½–¾-inch slices
Oil for frying

1. Mix egg with milk, salt and pepper.
2. Dip slices of eggplant in egg mixture and sauté in oil in a heavy skillet, browning well.

*Variation No. 1—Dip slices in sesame seed before browning.*
*Variation No. 2—After the first side is brown, turn and sprinkle with crumbled blue cheese.*

# GREEN BEAN AND EGGPLANT CASSEROLE

1 medium eggplant, peeled and cut in
    1-inch slices
1 egg, slightly beaten with
    2 tablespoons water
1½ cups fresh tomatoes, peeled and
    cut in large pieces
½ teaspoon marjoram
2 tablespoons instant flour
½ pound sharp American cheese,
    grated
  Salt and pepper
2 cups cooked green beans

1. Dip eggplant slices in egg mixture. Brown in a little hot oil. Set aside.

2. Combine tomatoes with marjoram and instant flour.

3. In a shallow 1½-quart casserole put a layer of eggplant; sprinkle with salt and pepper; pour over half of the tomatoes, then half the green beans and half the cheese. Repeat.

4. Bake in a 350° oven until cooked through.

# OPEN EGGPLANT SANDWICH

1 English muffin, split
2 slices sautéed eggplant Parmesan
2 slices tomato
2 1-ounce slices sharp American cheese

1. Toast muffin halves.
2. Place a slice of eggplant on muffin. Place slice of tomato on top of eggplant. Sprinkle with salt.
3. Cut slice of cheese in half and crisscross over tomato.
4. Place under broiler and broil until cheese is melted and brown.

# EGGPLANT CREOLE

2 medium onions, chopped
½ cup chopped celery
1 green pepper, chopped
¼ cup peanut oil
2 tomatoes, cut in chunks
1 unpeeled eggplant, cut in chunks
⅛ teaspoon garlic powder
1 teaspoon salt
Pepper to taste

1. Sauté onion, celery and peppers until brown in hot oil in a heavy skillet.
2. Add remaining ingredients, mix well. Cover and cook 20–30 minutes.

# BAKED LENTILS

2 tablespoons peanut oil
1 medium onion, chopped
1 cup dry lentils
1 teaspoon salt
1 cup stewed tomatoes, broken up
2 cups water
½ cup mashed potatoes
1 egg, slightly beaten
1 teaspoon poultry seasoning

1. Sauté onion in oil until brown. Add lentils, salt, tomatoes and water. Simmer about 1 hour or until done, adding more water if necessary.

2. Combine potatoes, egg and poultry seasoning. Mix with lentils.

3. Put mixture into a greased baking dish and bake 30 minutes in a 350° oven.

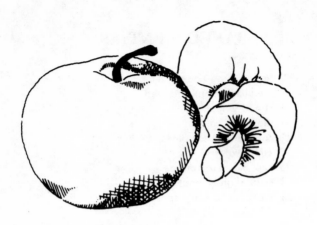

# STUFFED MUSHROOMS

8 large mushrooms
2 tablespoons butter or margarine
2 tablespoons minced onion
¼ cup fine dry bread crumbs
1 teaspoon dried parsley flakes
½ teaspoon oregano
  Dash of garlic salt
½ teaspoon salt
2 tablespoons grated Parmesan cheese
¼ cup sour cream

1. Remove stems from mushrooms. Brush caps with •melted butter. Chop stems fine.

2. Sauté onion and the chopped stems in butter about 5 minutes. Add remaining ingredients.

3. Fill mushroom caps with crumb mixture. Bake in a 375° oven about 20 minutes.

# MUSHROOM FILLING FOR CRÊPES

½ pound fresh mushrooms, chopped fine
2 tablespoons butter or margarine
2 tablespoons instant flour
2 tablespoons sour cream
1 teaspoon finely chopped chives
½ teaspoon salt

1. Sauté mushrooms a few minutes in butter or margarine. Sprinkle flour over and stir well until mixture thickens.
2. Add sour cream, chives and salt and cook a few minutes longer.
3. Put a spoonful on a crêpe; roll to enclose filling.
4. Heat in oven and serve with mushroom sauce. (See section on Sauces.)

# FRIED ONIONS AND APPLES

2 tablespoons butter or margarine
1 large onion, sliced
2 large cooking apples, peeled and
    sliced
1 tablespoon brown sugar
Dash salt

1. Melt butter in a heavy skillet.
2. Add onions and sauté five minutes. Add apples. Sprinkle with sugar and salt.
3. Brown slightly and cover. Cook over low heat until apples are soft but not mushy.

# ONIONS AND GREEN BEANS SUPREME

    2 tablespoons butter or margarine
    2 tablespoons flour
    ½ teaspoon dried dill weed
    ½ cup liquid drained from beans
    ½ cup sour cream
    2 cups cooked or canned green beans,
        drained
    1 buffet can small onions, drained
      Salt and pepper to taste
    2 teaspoons vinegar

1. Melt butter in double boiler; add flour and dill weed. Add reserved bean liquid and vinegar, stirring until thickened.

2. Add sour cream and vegetables and season to taste. Heat over a low heat, stirring occasionally, taking care not to break up vegetables.

# ONION PIE

1 9-inch pastry-lined pie pan
3 cups sliced onion
3 tablespoons butter
1½ cups milk, scalded
2 eggs, slightly beaten
1 teaspoon salt

1. Bake pie shell at 400° for 10 minutes.
2. Sauté onions in butter until golden. Turn into pie shell.
3. Add milk gradually to eggs. Add salt. Pour over onions.
4. Bake in 350° oven until firm in the middle.

# LEEK PIE

Make like onion pie, substituting leeks for onions.

# CHEESE-SCALLOPED ONIONS

4 medium onions, sliced in ½-inch
    slices
⅓ cup milk
2 eggs, slightly beaten
1 can Cheddar cheese soup
1 cup cheese puff snacks

1. Separate onion slices into rings and cook 10 minutes in boiling salted water. Drain well. Place in shallow buttered casserole.

2. Add milk and eggs to soup. Pour over onions. Sprinkle cheese puffs on top.

3. Bake in 350° oven until a knife inserted in the middle comes out clean, about 35 minutes.

# HELEN'S SCALLOPED ONIONS

8 medium onions, cut in ¼-inch slices
2 slices of lemon
½ cup heavy cream
1 cup soft bread crumbs
2 tablespoons butter

1. Separate onions into rings. Boil in salted water with lemon slices until tender. Drain.

2. Place onion slices in buttered shallow baking dish. Pour cream over.

3. Sprinkle crumbs on top and dot with butter.

4. Place under broiler until crumbs are brown or in a hot oven, if you prefer.

# SPLIT PEAS AND TOMATOES

1 cup green split peas
2 tablespoons chopped onion
1 teaspoon salt
2 tablespoons butter
3 tablespoons flour
⅔ cup milk
    Salt and pepper
2 cups stewed tomatoes, drained
1 cup cooked rice
1 cup buttered bread crumbs

1. Soak the peas overnight in water. Drain and cook in fresh water with the onion and salt. Cook until tender. Drain, reserving ⅓ cup of the liquid.

2. Melt butter; add flour and make a roux. Add to the reserved split pea liquid and milk, stirring constantly. Add salt and pepper to taste.

3. In a buttered baking dish, place alternate layers of peas, sauce, tomatoes and rice.

4. Sprinkle buttered crumbs over top and bake at 350° about 30 minutes.

# PEAS AND ONIONS IN MUSHROOM SAUCE

1 can condensed mushroom soup
2 cups cooked frozen peas, drained
1 buffet can boiled onions, drained
½ can sliced mushrooms, drained
2 tablespoons toasted slivered almonds

1. Heat mushroom soup in double boiler.
2. Combine vegetables; mix with soup and heat.
3. Pour into serving dish. Garnish with toasted slivered almonds.

# PEAS AND CELERY IN ALMOND SAUCE

2 cups cooked peas, drained
⅔ cup cooked celery, drained
3 tablespoons butter or margarine
3 tablespoons flour
1 cup milk, scalded
½ cup liquid from peas and celery
1 teaspoon instant onion flakes
½ teaspoon salt
½ teaspoon MSG
¼ cup toasted, slivered almonds

1. Make a roux of butter or margarine and flour. Add to scalded milk with the vegetable juice. Stir constantly until thick. Add onion, salt, MSG and half the almonds.
2. Combine vegetables and sauce, mixing carefully. Heat thoroughly. Pour into serving dish and top with remaining almonds.

# PEPPERS STUFFED WITH CORN

6 medium green peppers
¼ cup chopped green pepper
2 tablespoons chopped onion
1 cup corn, cut from cob
2 cups soft bread crumbs
2 medium tomatoes, peeled and
    chopped
  Salt and pepper to taste
½ teaspoon dry mustard
1 cup grated Cheddar cheese
2 eggs, slightly beaten

1. Remove stem end of peppers; seed and steam or parboil until they turn a dull green.

2. Sauté chopped pepper and onion in butter until tender.

3. Add remaining ingredients and mix well. Taste for seasoning. Fill peppers.

4. Put filled peppers in a baking dish with water about ¼-inch deep.

5. Bake about 30–35 minutes in a 350° oven.

# HASHED CREAMED POTATOES

2 tablespoons butter
2 tablespoons flour
1 cup milk, scalded
2½ cups cooked potatoes, chopped
        very fine
    Salt and pepper to taste
½ cup buttered crumbs

1. Melt the butter; blend in flour and whip into scalded milk. Cook until it thickens.

2. Add potatoes to sauce and season with salt and pepper.

3. Put mixture into buttered casserole and top with buttered crumbs. Bake in a 350° oven until brown and heated through.

*Note: For best results, cook potatoes the day before you wish to use them.*

# AU GRATIN POTATOES

1. Prepare hashed creamed potatoes, adding ½ cup grated sharp cheese to the sauce.

2. Add ¼ cup grated cheese to the crumbs before sprinkling on top of potato mixture.

# PERKY'S POTATO DUMPLINGS

        2 cups potatoes, cooked the day before
            and riced and chilled
        2 tablespoons flour
        1 tablespoon farina
        1 teaspoon salt
        1 egg, slightly beaten
        1 tablespoon melted butter or
            margarine
        ⅛ teaspoon nutmeg
            Flour to roll, as needed
            Chopped parsley

1. Combine all ingredients. Mix thoroughly. Shape into balls, roll lightly in flour and chill.

2. Drop into gently boiling salted water. Cover and cook 10–15 minutes.

3. Remove from water. Garnish with fresh chopped parsley. Serve hot.

*Note: A few croutons may be placed in the center of each dumpling if desired.*

*Since the moisture content of potatoes varies, you may wish to "test-cook" one dumpling first. If it doesn't hold together, more flour may be added.*

*If you don't have a potato ricer, put potatoes through a food mill or mash until free from lumps.*

# ARMENIAN POTATOES

¼ cup peanut oil
4 cups diced raw potatoes
4 tablespoons tomato paste
½ cup water
1½ teaspoons salt
1 teaspoon paprika
1 large onion, grated
1 tablespoon dried parsley flakes

1. Mix all ingredients together. Put into a greased casserole.
2. Bake, covered, at 325° for about 1 hour.

# POTATO–CORN PIE

Pastry for 9-inch, 2-crust pie
1 cup raw potatoes cut in ¼-inch cubes
2 cups cooked, whole-kernel corn
Salt and pepper
4 tablespoons heavy cream
½ teaspoon dried parsley flakes

1. Combine potatoes and corn. Turn into pastry-lined pie pan. Sprinkle with salt and pepper.
2. Pour heavy cream over vegetables. Sprinkle with parsley.
3. Cover with pastry. Brush with cream.
4. Bake in a 375° oven until well browned, about 40 minutes.

# POTATOES AND SWISS CHEESE EN CASSEROLE

1½ cups dairy sour cream
2 tablespoons instant onion
1 teaspoon MSG
1½ teaspoons salt
1½ cups grated Swiss cheese
4 cups diced cooked potatoes
¼ cup melted butter or margarine
¼ cup crushed cornflakes

1. Combine sour cream with instant onion, MSG, salt and the grated cheese.

2. In a buttered casserole put a layer of potatoes and cover with the sour cream mixture. Repeat.

3. Top with cornflakes mixed with melted butter or margarine.

4. Bake in a 375° oven until hot and brown.

# ELECTRIC SKILLET QUICK ESCALLOPED POTATOES

2 cups milk
2 tablespoons butter
2 teaspoons instant onion
3 cups sliced raw potatoes
2 tablespoons flour—instant type
1 teaspoon salt
⅛ teaspoon pepper
1 tablespoon chopped parsley

1. Heat milk in skillet, 225°. Add butter and instant onion flakes.

2. Slice potatoes; rinse and drain. Add flour, salt and pepper. Put in skillet. Stir and cover.

3. Cook until potatoes are tender. Turn into serving dish and sprinkle with chopped parsley.

## EASY POTATO CASSEROLE

    1 cup dairy sour cream
    ¾ cup milk
    2 tablespoons grated onion
    1 teaspoon dried dill weed
    2 teaspoons salt
    ¼ teaspoon pepper
    5 medium cooked potatoes, diced
    2 tablespoons dry bread crumbs
    2 tablespoons grated American cheese
      Paprika

1. Mix sour cream, milk, onion, salt, pepper and dill weed.

2. Put half the potatoes in a 1½-quart casserole. Add half the sour cream mixture. Repeat.

3. Combine bread crumbs and grated cheese. Sprinkle over top and sprinkle liberally with paprika.

4. Bake in 350° oven until well heated and browned.

# STEWED POTATOES

4 medium potatoes
1 medium onion, chopped
1 small green pepper
1 tablespoon butter
  Salt and pepper to taste

1. Peel and slice potatoes as for escalloped potatoes.
2. Sauté onion and pepper in butter until brown in a heavy skillet.
3. Add potatoes, salt and pepper and water to cover.
4. Cover skillet and cook until potatoes are done, stirring several times to thicken the liquid.

# SWISS SKILLET POTATOES

6 medium potatoes, sliced thin
¼ cup melted butter
  Salt and pepper
1 cup grated Swiss cheese

1. Let potatoes stand in cold water ½ hour. Drain and dry between paper towels.
2. Butter bottom of a heavy skillet. Place a layer of potato slices, overlapping, to cover the bottom of skillet. Brush with melted butter. Sprinkle with salt and pepper and grated cheese. Repeat layers, ending with potatoes.
3. Cook over low heat, covered, until potatoes are done. Turn upside down on serving plate. Cut in wedges.

"A small unkindness is a great offence."

**Hannah More**

# SPICED YAMS

1⅓ cups sugar
1 cup water
2 2-inch pieces stick cinnamon
¼ teaspoon nutmeg
Dash of salt
2 tablespoons lemon juice
Grated rind of one lemon
6 yams, cooked and peeled
2 tablespoons butter or margarine

1. Combine sugar, water, spices, lemon juice and rind. Bring to a boil and cook over low heat for 5 minutes.

2. Place yams in a casserole and pour syrup over. Dot with butter or margarine.

3. Bake in a 350° oven about 30 minutes, basting with syrup several times.

# LILLIAN'S SWEET POTATO AND PINEAPPLE CASSEROLE

6 large sweet potatoes, peeled and
   cooked
½ cup margarine or butter
4 tablespoons flour
¼ teaspoon salt
¾ cup light brown sugar
1 cup pineapple juice (drained from
   the pineapple)
6 slices canned pineapple, diced

1. Slice sweet potatoes in ¼-inch slices.

2. Melt margarine and add the flour, salt and brown sugar, which have been mixed together. Add the pineapple juice and cook until thick, stirring constantly.

3. In a buttered casserole, alternate layers of sweet potatoes and pineapple. Pour pineapple sauce over all.

4. Bake in 350° oven 30–35 minutes.

# POTATO–TURNIP CAKES

1 cup mashed turnips
1 cup mashed potatoes
4 tablespoons instant flour
1 egg, slightly beaten
1 teaspoon salt
2 teaspoons finely chopped chives

1. Combine turnips and potatoes. Add remaining ingredients and mix well.
2. Shape into cakes and sauté in vegetable oil in a heavy skillet, turning once.

*Note: If you have an ice cream scoop, you can scoop mixture directly into skillet.*

# EAST INDIAN STYLE POTATOES AND PEAS

2 tablespoons peanut oil
2 cups cooked diced potatoes
1 cup cooked peas
Salt and pepper
¼ teaspoon tumeric
½ teaspoon curry powder

1. Heat oil in skillet.
2. Combine peas and potatoes with seasonings.
3. Brown in oil, stirring carefully so as not to break up the peas.

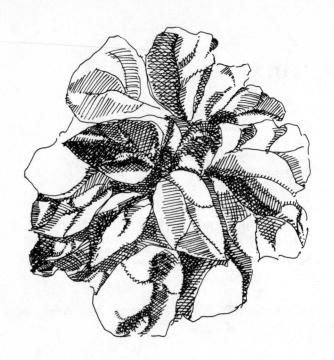

## SAVORY STUFFED POTATOES

*For each medium baked potato:*

1 teaspoon minced onion
1 teaspoon butter
1 tablespoon milk
¼ teaspoon poultry seasoning
¼ teaspoon salt

1. Sauté onion in the butter until golden.
2. Scoop potatoes from shell and mash. Add milk, seasonings and onion. Taste for seasonings; add more salt if necessary.
3. Pile back into shells, dust with paprika and put in a hot oven, 400°, to brown.

# SAUERKRAUT WITH GREEN GRAPES

1 1-pound can sauerkraut, drained
½ cup green grapes, cut in half
¾ cup white wine
2 tablespoons butter or margarine

1. Put sauerkraut in saucepan. Add remaining ingredients.
2. Cover and simmer 25–30 minutes.

# SPINACH PUFF

1 10-ounce package frozen spinach
1 cup cooked rice
1 teaspoon instant onion flakes
½ teaspoon salt
2 eggs, separated

1. Cook spinach five minutes. Drain well.
2. Add spinach to rice with egg yolks, onion flakes and salt. Mix well.
3. Beat egg whites until stiff but not dry. Fold spinach mixture gently into egg whites.
4. Pour into greased casserole and bake in a 350° oven until a knife inserted in the middle comes out clean—about 30 minutes.

# SPINACH LOAF

1  10-ounce package frozen chopped
   spinach
2  tablespoons butter, melted
3  tablespoons flour
⅛  teaspoon pepper
1  teaspoon salt
1  cup milk, scalded
2  eggs, slightly beaten

1. Cook spinach. Drain well.
2. Make a roux of butter, flour and seasonings. Add to milk to make a cream sauce.
3. Combine eggs, cream sauce and spinach.
4. Pour into a buttered casserole.
5. Bake at 350° until a knife inserted in the center comes out clean, about 35–40 minutes.

# CREAMY SPINACH

1 10-ounce package washed spinach
2 tablespoons butter or margarine
2 tablespoons flour
  Few gratings nutmeg
  Salt and pepper to taste

1. Cook spinach in small amount of boiling salted water until barely tender. Drain and chop, reserving 6 tablespoons liquid.

2. Melt butter or margarine; add flour to make a roux, add reserved liquid, and blend into drained spinach. Cook over low heat until thickened. Add nutmeg.

# CRANBERRY ACORN SQUASH

2 acorn squash
4 tablespoons melted butter or
    margarine
1 cup whole cranberry sauce
½ teaspoon nutmeg
½ teaspoon grated orange rind

1. Cut squash in half lengthwise; remove seeds; brush with butter or margarine and place cut side down on a greased baking pan. Bake about 45 minutes at 350°.

2. Turn squash hollow side up, and fill with cranberry sauce mixed with nutmeg and grated orange rind. Bake until tender, about 15 minutes.

# ACORN SQUASH FILLED WITH APPLESAUCE

2 acorn squash, cut in half and seeded
2 tablespoons butter or margarine,
   melted
1 cup applesauce
2 tablespoons brown sugar
   Juice and grated rind of ½ lemon
¼ teaspoon cinnamon
¼ teaspoon nutmeg
¼ cup raisins

1. Brush insides of squash with butter or margarine. Invert on a greased baking pan and bake at 350° for 45 minutes.

2. Combine applesauce with remaining ingredients. Fill centers of squash with applesauce mixture and return to oven. Bake another 20 minutes or until squash is well done and filling hot.

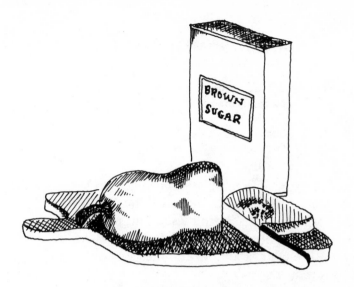

## GLAZED BUTTERNUT SQUASH

1 2-pound butternut squash
6 tablespoons brown sugar
2 tablespoons dark corn syrup
4 tablespoons water
¼ cup melted butter or margarine
½ teaspoon cinnamon
¼ teaspoon ginger

1. Slice squash in 1½-inch slices, removing the seeds and skin.

2. Steam squash slices in a small amount of water on a rack for about 12 minutes or until nearly done.

3. Place squash slices on a buttered shallow baking pan.

4. Combine sugar, corn syrup, water, butter and spices. Pour over squash. Bake in a 400° oven until tender and glazed—about 20 minutes.

# BAKED SUMMER SQUASH

6–8-inch summer squash
Melted margarine or butter
Dill weed
Salt
Paprika

1. Split squash lengthwise and place on greased oven-proof platter. Brush with melted butter.
2. Sprinkle with salt, dill weed and paprika.
3. Cover tightly with aluminum foil. Bake in a 375° oven until tender, about 45 minutes, uncovering after 30 minutes to brown.

# BAKED WINTER SQUASH

4 cups winter squash, cut in ¾-inch
      cubes
¼ cup brown sugar
1 teaspoon salt
1 teaspoon cinnamon
½ cup heavy cream

1. Put squash in buttered baking dish. Mix sugar, salt and cinnamon and sprinkle over squash.
2. Pour cream over. Cover dish and bake in a 350° oven about an hour until squash is tender.

# SUMMER SQUASH BAKE

1 pound yellow summer squash, cooked
   and drained
⅓ cup fine saltine crumbs
2 tablespoons butter or margarine,
   melted
½ cup diced celery
¼ cup chopped onion
2 eggs, slightly beaten
1 teaspoon dried dill weed
1 teaspoon salt
1½ cups milk, scalded

1. Add cracker crumbs to squash.

2. Sauté celery and onion in melted butter or margarine for five minutes. Add to squash.

3. Add eggs, blend and add dill weed and salt. Add milk and pour into buttered baking dish.

4. Bake 45 minutes in 375° oven or until a knife inserted in middle comes out clean.

# YELLOW AND GREEN SQUASH MEDLEY

2 small zucchini squash
2 small yellow summer squash
2 teaspoons salt
1 tablespoon butter or margarine
1 teaspoon sugar
1 tablespoon instant onion flakes
6 tablespoons water

1. Wash squash and slice into ¼-inch thick slices.
2. Put in heavy saucepan with remaining ingredients.
3. Cover pan tightly and cook until tender over low heat.

# ORIENTAL CITRUS SQUASH

2 acorn squash
½ cup orange marmalade
2 teaspoons candied ginger, slivered
1 tablespoon lemon juice

1. Prepare squash as for Cranberry Acorn Squash.
2. When first 45 minutes of baking is completed, fill with mixture of marmalade mixed with slivered ginger and lemon juice.
3. Bake an additional 15 minutes or until squash is tender.

## FRENCH-FRIED SQUASH

Butternut squash, cut in ¾-inch slices

1. Parboil squash slices for 5 minutes in salted boiling water. Drain.
2. Deep fry squash in 375° fat until brown. Drain and sprinkle with salt.

# ROSEMARY ZUCCHINI SQUASH

1¼–1½ pounds zucchini squash
4 tablespoons chopped onion
2 tablespoons butter or margarine
½ cup canned tomato-mushroom sauce
1 teaspoon salt
¼ teaspoon rosemary

1. Wash squash and cut in ¼-inch slices.
2. Sauté onion in butter until golden.
3. Combine squash, tomato sauce, sautéed onions, salt and rosemary. Cover and cook until tender, about fifteen minutes.

# MAIZIE'S SQUASH CAKES

2 cups cooked and drained yellow
    summer squash
1 egg, slightly beaten
4 tablespoons instant flour
1 teaspoon grated onion
½ teaspoon salt
  Dash pepper
  Oil for frying

1. Mix all ingredients except oil.
2. Heat oil in heavy skillet. Drop squash mixture by spoonfuls into hot fat. Brown on each side, turning once. Serve hot.

# FRIED TOMATOES WITH CREAM GRAVY

2 large tomatoes, cut in thirds
½ cup cornmeal
2 tablespoons margarine or butter
2 tablespoons flour
1 cup milk
  Salt and pepper

1. Slice tomatoes; sprinkle with salt and pepper and dip in cornmeal.

2. Sauté in butter in a heavy skillet until brown. Remove to a hot platter.

3. Add flour to drippings in skillet to make a roux. Add milk, stirring constantly, to make a sauce. Taste for seasoning.

4. Serve tomatoes on toast if desired, with sauce poured over.

# STUFFED TOMATOES

4 medium tomatoes
2 tablespoons butter
1 tablespoon onion, minced
1 cup soft bread crumbs
1 egg
¼ teaspoon basil
½ teaspoon salt
2 tablespoons grated Parmesan cheese

1. Cut a thin slice from stem end of tomatoes. Scoop out and reserve the pulp. Invert tomatoes while preparing filling.

2. Sauté onion in butter until golden. Add to the bread crumbs with seasonings, egg and tomato pulp.

3. Fill tomatoes with bread mixture. Sprinkle top with cheese and place in buttered shallow pan.

4. Bake about 30 minutes at 350°.

# DOUBLE CHEESE-BROILED TOMATOES

Medium tomatoes, cut in half
Melted butter or margarine
Basil
Salt and pepper
Sliced Cheddar cheese
Grated Parmesan cheese

1. Brush tomatoes with melted butter.
2. Sprinkle with salt, pepper and basil.
3. Place a small slice of Cheddar cheese on tomato and sprinkle with grated Parmesan cheese.
4. Place under broiler, or in a 400° oven until cheese melts and tomatoes are heated through.

# TOMATO–CORN MEDLEY

1 tablespoon oil
½ cup chopped green pepper
½ cup chopped onion
1 cup cooked corn
1 cup tomatoes, peeled and coarsely
    chopped
½ teaspoon salt
Dash of pepper

1. Put oil in a heavy skillet. Sauté onions and peppers five minutes.
2. Add corn, tomatoes and seasonings and cook five minutes longer. Serve on toast or over rice.

# TOMATO QUICHE

1 9-inch pie shell
1 cup drained cooked Italian plum
   tomatoes
¼ teaspoon basil
1 tablespoon instant onion flakes
½ cup grated Swiss cheese
½ cup grated Cheddar cheese
2 eggs, slightly beaten
1 cup cream
1 teaspoon salt

1. Bake the pie shell in a 375° oven for 10 minutes.
2. Place tomatoes in pie shell. Sprinkle with basil and onion flakes.
3. Spread cheese over tomatoes.
4. Add cream to eggs. Add salt and pour over cheese.
5. Bake in a 375° oven 40–45 minutes until set. Cool 5 minutes before cutting.

*Note: Half this recipe will fill a 6¾-inch pie shell. If you are a weight watcher, make a "crustless" quiche, putting the mixture into a greased pie pan in the same manner.*

# TOMATO SCRAPPLE

1¼ cups stewed tomatoes
¼ cup chopped onion
¼ cup grated carrot
½ cup cornmeal
1 teaspoon sugar
1 teaspoon salt
Dash of pepper
½ cup chopped, roasted peanuts

1. Add carrots and seasonings to tomatoes and bring to a boil in top of double boiler. Very slowly add corn-meal, stirring constantly.

2. Set top of double boiler over hot water and cook slowly 1 hour. Stir in peanuts.

3. Pour into oiled pan. Cool and refrigerate until firm.

4. Slice and sauté in oil until brown and crisp.

*Note: Peanuts may be omitted.*

# TOMATOES AND OATMEAL

1 cup stewed tomatoes
1 cup boiling water
1 teaspoon salt
Dash of pepper
½ teaspoon instant onion flakes
½ teaspoon dried parsley flakes
½ teaspoon sugar
1 cup oatmeal
3 tablespoons melted margarine or
    butter

1.  Add tomatoes to water; bring to a boil. Add seasonings.

2.  Slowly add oatmeal to tomato mixture, stirring constantly. Cook slowly, until dry. Add margarine or butter.

# TOMATO PILAF

1 cup raw rice
2 tablespoons peanut oil
2 cups hot stewed tomatoes
1 teaspoon salt
2 cups boiling water

1.  Brown the rice in peanut oil in a heavy pot or skillet.

2.  Lower heat. Add tomatoes, salt and boiling water. Cook over low heat until rice is tender and all the liquid absorbed.

# ANN'S TOMATO–BEET CASSEROLE

1¼ cups cooked diced beets, drained
1¼ cups stewed tomatoes
¼ cup grated American cheese
Salt and pepper
1 cup day-old bread crumbs
2 tablespoons butter or margarine,
melted

1. In a buttered casserole put half the beets, then half the tomatoes and half the cheese. Sprinkle with salt and pepper. Add half the bread crumbs and drizzle with half the butter or margarine. Repeat.
2. Bake in a 350° oven until brown on top—about 20 minutes.

# SOUFFLÉ-TOPPED TOMATOES

4 small tomatoes
1 egg, separated
¼ cup mayonnaise
1 tablespoon sweet pickle relish
¼ cup grated Cheddar cheese

1. Cut tomatoes in half and place on greased oven-proof platter.
2. Combine egg yolk, mayonnaise, relish and cheese.
3. Beat egg white until stiff but not dry and fold into mayonnaise mixture. Pour over and around tomatoes.
4. Bake in a 350° oven about 20–25 minutes until mixture is cooked through.

*Note: It would not be advisable to reduce this recipe unless you use the whole egg yolk and discard half the beaten egg white.*

# TURNIP SOUFFLÉ

4 eggs, separated
2 cups cooked mashed seasoned turnips
1 can condensed Cheddar cheese soup
½ teaspoon salt

1. Beat egg whites with salt until stiff but not dry.
2. Beat egg yolks until thick and lemony. Add to turnips.
3. Fold egg whites into turnip mixture. Pour into a 2-quart baking dish, buttered on the bottom.
4. Bake at 350° until a knife inserted in the middle comes out clean, about 35 minutes.

*Note: Mushroom soup may be substituted for Cheddar cheese soup.*

# TURNIPS WITH CHEESE SAUCE

4 cups diced turnips
1 can condensed Cheddar cheese soup
¼ teaspoon savory

1. Cook turnips until tender. Drain.
2. Heat Cheddar cheese soup with savory.
3. Add soup mixture to turnips. Let stand over low heat a few minutes to combine flavors.

# Cheese

The main good that is being accomplished by the propaganda for "humane slaughter," as well as that for "humane traps," is that it awakens many to the atrocious cruelty involved in the obtaining of flesh food and fur. Many consecrated humanitarians urge that these slayings be done "in the kindliest way that a noble humanity can devise." I wish to submit that a "noble humanity" will not devise ways of doing IGNOBLE and INHUMAN acts, and that "humane slaughter" will never be seriously undertaken by a race that demands the wholesale slaughtering of innocent creatures for a food which no well-informed person can today regard as a necessity. There is now no divergence of opinion on this, among the acknowledged authorities, modern ideas being well summed up in a report of the "Life Extension Institute" which states that animal proteins are not necessary for man's growth or development since these proteins are fully substituted in food not animal.

Emarel Freshel

# BAKED CHEESE AND NOODLES

4 ounces uncooked medium noodles
2 tablespoons butter or margarine
2 tablespoons chopped onion
2 tablespoons chopped celery
2 tablespoons chopped green pepper
1 teaspoon salt
  Dash of pepper
½ teaspoon MSG
1 tablespoon flour
⅔ cup milk
1 cup cottage cheese
1 tablespoon lemon juice
1 teaspoon dried parsley flakes
2 eggs, slightly beaten

1. Cook noodles in boiling salted water about 5 minutes. Rinse and drain well.

2. Melt butter or margarine in heavy pot. Sauté onion, celery and pepper until tender.

3. Add salt, pepper, MSG and flour and blend. Stir in milk to make a smooth sauce.

4. Combine noodles, sauce, cottage cheese, parsley flakes, lemon juice and eggs. Pour into a buttered baking dish. Bake 30–40 minutes in a 350° oven until firm in the middle.

# CHEESE STRATA

8 slices dark diet bread
1 cup shredded Cheddar cheese
½ teaspoon dry mustard
½ teaspoon salt
½ teaspoon dry basil
1 teaspoon instant onion flakes
4 eggs, slightly beaten
1½ cups milk

1. Put 4 slices of bread in a buttered shallow baking dish. Sprinkle cheese over and top with remaining slices.

2. Mix mustard, salt, basil and onion flakes. Add eggs and milk.

3. Pour milk mixture over bread and chill in the refrigerator an hour.

4. Bake in a 350° oven about 1 hour or until a knife comes out clean when inserted in the middle.

# COTTAGE CHEESE AND VEGETABLES IN CASSEROLE

2 cups cooked, mixed vegetables, drained
1 cup cream-style cottage cheese
2 tablespoons chopped pimientos
2 teaspoons instant onion flakes
2 teaspoons minced parsley
¼ teaspoon MSG
2 eggs, slightly beaten
½ teaspoon salt
½ cup milk

1. Place vegetables in a buttered baking dish.

2. Add onion, pimientos, MSG and parsley to cottage cheese and spread over vegetables.

3. Combine eggs, salt and milk and pour over cheese and vegetables; set baking dish in a pan of hot water.

4. Bake at 350° for 30 minutes or until set. Let stand about 10 minutes to firm up before serving.

# CHEESE–RICE FRITTERS

1 cup cooked rice
1 egg, slightly beaten
½ cup grated American cheese (sharp)
1 tablespoon milk
1 teaspoon prepared mustard
1 teaspoon Worcestershire sauce
½ teaspoon salt
¼ teaspoon MSG
¼ teaspoon paprika
   Fine dry bread crumbs

1. Mix all ingredients except bread crumbs.
2. Shape into balls, roll in bread crumbs and fry in deep fat, 375°, until brown.
3. Serve with spiced applesauce.

# CHEESE PUDDING

1 cup soft bread crumbs
1 cup grated sharp Cheddar cheese
2 cups milk, scalded
2 eggs, slightly beaten
½ teaspoon dry mustard
1 teaspoon Worcestershire sauce
1 teaspoon salt
   Dash of pepper

1. Mix the bread crumbs and cheese together and put into a buttered baking dish.

2. Add milk gradually to eggs which have been mixed with seasonings.

3. Pour milk mixture over crumbs and cheese. Bake in a 350° oven until it is firm like a custard—about 40 minutes.

## COTTAGE CHEESE PANCAKES

2 eggs
1 cup creamed cottage cheese
¼ cup instant flour
½ teaspoon baking powder
1 tablespoon sugar
1 tablespoon lemon juice
½ teaspoon grated lemon rind
2 tablespoons melted butter or
    margarine

1. Put all ingredients in blender and blend until smooth.

2. Cook on greased griddle until golden brown on both sides.

3. Serve with preserves.

"If the Creator should ask for a report on the dominion which He is said to have given Man, would we not be embarrassed? Doubtless the Adam and Cain in us would be quick to gloss over the fact that we have become too busy to remember this responsibility. But if He from whom no secrets are hid should take the testimony of the creatures themselves, what would they tell Him of our stewardship? Something of friendship and partnership with the dog, cat, horse and tropical animals; but an increasing amount of exploitation and treachery with the livestock upon whose flesh itself we have design."

Henry Bailey Stevens

# Salads

"We have tried to operate a church and a schoolhouse at one end of the street and a slaughterhouse at the other; to fill our minds with kindness and our stomachs with tortured flesh; to teach peace and eat like beasts of prey. But we have overlooked the moral in the story of Diomedes. Each generation has run amok and torn us to pieces in return for the ugly lies which it has been taught —viz. that animals must be killed for food and people for military objectives."

Henry Bailey Stevens

# DEVILED EGGS

4 hard-cooked eggs, cut in half
Butter
1 tablespoon mayonnaise
1 teaspoon catsup
¼ teaspoon prepared mustard
¼ teaspoon sugar
1 teaspoon vinegar
¼ teaspoon salt


1. Mash egg yolks until free from lumps. Add almost an equal lump of butter at room temperature.

2. Add remaining ingredients to egg yolks and blend well.

3. Pile yolks into whites, using spoon or pastry tube.

4. Garnish as you wish—parsley, paprika, capers, olives, chopped walnuts are suggestions.

# ITALIAN VEGETABLE SALAD

1 cup diced cooked beets
1 cup diced cooked carrots
1 cup diced raw celery
½ cup cooked peas
½ cup diced, peeled cucumbers
¼ cup mayonnaise
2 tablespoons sour cream
1 tablespoon lemon juice
½ teaspoon sugar
½ teaspoon salt

1. Combine vegetables.
2. Mix mayonnaise, sour cream, lemon juice, sugar and salt. Pour over vegetables and combine lightly.
3. Serve in a lettuce-lined salad bowl.

# GREEN MEDLEY SALAD

2 cups cooked lima beans
2 cups cooked peas
2 cups cooked green beans
French dressing

1. Combine beans and peas.
2. Pour your favorite French dressing over and marinate several hours.
3. Drain and serve on salad greens.

"I do not see how it is possible that so many good people remain meat-eaters."

Tolstoy

## BEET, BEAN AND PEA SALAD

1 cup cooked diced beets
1 cup cooked green beans, cut in
    1-inch lengths
1 cup cooked peas
¼ cup mayonnaise
1 teaspoon red wine vinegar
½ teaspoon sugar
Salt to taste

1. Drain vegetables and chill well.
2. Combine remaining ingredients and add to vegetables.
3. Serve in a lettuce-lined salad bowl.

# PILLY'S SALAD

1 head of lettuce
½ pound fresh mushrooms
½ pound seedless green grapes
½ cup French dressing
2 tablespoons red wine vinegar
1 box cherry tomatoes


1. Wash lettuce, drain and tear in bite-size pieces.
2. Wash mushrooms and slice thin. Wash and drain green grapes.
3. Combine grapes, mushrooms and lettuce with the French dressing mixed with vinegar. Use more or less dressing depending on size of lettuce. Put in salad bowl.
4. Garnish with cherry tomatoes.

# WALDORF SALAD DELUXE

2 cups diced eating apples
2 slices pineapple, cut in pieces
1 cup red grapes, split and seeded
½ cup chopped celery
2 tablespoons coarsely chopped walnuts
6 tablespoons Waldorf or fruit salad
    dressing

1. If apples have nice red skins, do not peel. Combine
all ingredients.

2. Place in salad bowl lined with greens. Serve well
chilled.

# PICKLED BEETS

1 can sliced beets
1 small onion sliced in rings
¼ cup sugar
¼ cup cider vinegar
1 teaspoon mixed pickling spice

1. Drain beets, putting liquid in saucepan.
2. To beet juice add sugar, vinegar and spices.
3. Bring to a boil and pour over beets and onion rings.
4. Let stand until cool. Refrigerate and serve cold.

# TURNIP SLAW

½ teaspoon sugar
¼ teaspoon salt
2 teaspoons red wine vinegar
2 tablespoons mayonnaise
¼ cup sour cream
2 cups shredded raw turnips

1. Mix sugar, salt, vinegar, mayonnaise and sour cream until well blended.
2. Pour mayonnaise mixture over turnips and toss lightly to mix.
3. Serve in bowl lined with salad greens and sprinkle paprika over top.

## MARINATED CHICK PEAS

Cooked chick peas
Your favorite French dressing

1. Drain chick peas.
2. Place in a bowl and pour French dressing over to cover.
3. Let stand overnight. Use in mixed green salads.

# THREE-BEAN SALAD

    6 tablespoons oil
    ½ cup vinegar
    2 tablespoons sugar
      Few drops hot pepper sauce
      Salt and pepper to taste
    1 medium onion, sliced in rings
    1 1-pound can green beans
    1 1-pound can wax beans
    2 cups cooked baby lima beans


1. Make marinade of first five ingredients and pour over beans. Add onion.

2. Cover and let stand several hours; overnight is better. Turn occasionally with a wooden spoon.

3. Drain and put in a salad bowl lined with lettuce.

## KIDNEY BEAN SALAD

  2 cups cooked kidney beans
  ½ cup chopped celery
1½ teaspoons grated onion
  ¼ cup mayonnaise
  ½ teaspoon sugar
  1 tablespoon sweet pickle relish
  2 eggs, hard-cooked and coarsely
      chopped
  2 teaspoons red wine vinegar

1. Put beans in a colander and rinse with cold water. Drain well.

2. Combine remaining ingredients and add to beans. Chill well.

"Hast thou named all the birds without a gun?
Loved the woodroses and left it on its stalk?
At rich men's tables eaten bread and pulse?
Oh, be my friend, and teach me to be thine!"

Ralph Waldo Emerson

# Salad Dressings

# LOLA'S DRESSING FOR
# WALDORF SALAD

½ cup sugar
3 tablespoons flour
¼ teaspoon salt
1 cup water
3 tablespoons cider vinegar
¼ cup sour cream

1. Combine sugar, flour and salt in a saucepan.
2. Add water and bring to a boil. Cook for 2 minutes.
3. Remove from heat, add vinegar and cool.
4. Add sour cream and mix well.

*Note: This is also good on fruit salad.*

## ROSALIE'S FRENCH DRESSING

1 cup sugar
1 tablespoon salt
1 tablespoon paprika
1 cup cider vinegar
¾ cup catsup
½ cup salad oil

Combine all ingredients in a jar and shake well.

## BLUE CHEESE DRESSING

¼ cup blue cheese, at room temperature
½ cup mayonnaise
2 tablespoons milk
2 teaspoons red wine vinegar

1. Cream blue cheese well and add mayonnaise gradually.
2. Add milk until well blended.
3. Add vinegar slowly and stir until well blended.

# THOUSAND ISLAND DRESSING WITH CHICK PEAS

To each cup of Thousand Island dressing, add ½ cup of chick peas.

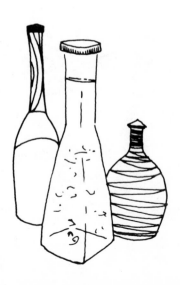

# BLUE CHEESE TOPPING

1 cup blue cheese
1 cup margarine or butter
⅛ teaspoon garlic powder
1 tablespoon prepared mustard
1 teaspoon Worcestershire sauce
⅛ teaspoon pepper

1. Bring margarine and cheese to room temperature.

2. Put all ingredients in bowl of mixer and beat until very smooth. Use your blender if you prefer.

3. Pack into small frozen juice cans. When well chilled, cut lid off can, push contents out and slice.

4. Good on broiled tomatoes, sautéed eggplant, or as a spread on toasted Italian bread or rolls as a "go-with" for soup or salad.

# FRUIT FRENCH DRESSING

   1 cup salad oil
   3 tablespoons lemon juice
   6 tablespoons orange juice
  ¼ cup pineapple juice
   1 cup vinegar
  ¾ teaspoon paprika
  ¾ teaspoon salt
1½ tablespoons confectioners' sugar
   1 tablespoon Worcestershire sauce
   3 tablespoons dried parsley flakes

Combine all ingredients in a jar and shake well.

# FRUIT SALAD DRESSING

¼ cup apricot nectar
¼ cup lemon juice
⅓ cup sugar
   Dash of salt
2 eggs, slightly beaten
¼ cup sour cream


1. Combine apricot nectar, lemon juice, sugar and salt in top of double boiler. Add eggs, blend well, and cook over hot water until the mixture coats the spoon. Cool.

2. Stir sour cream into mixture and chill.

# Sauces

"Thieves and enemies are not found among those that feed on maize—but sycophants and tyrants are produced from those who feed on flesh."

Diogenes

# EASY SAUCES

Canned condensed soups make wonderful easy sauces. Cream of mushroom, Cheddar cheese and celery are but a few.

To each can of soup add ½ cup of milk and heat. Add ½ cup grated Cheddar cheese if you wish.

To cheese sauce, add a bit of dry mustard or a dash of Worcestershire for an added fillip.

A dash of catsup is good in tomato-soup sauce.

# MORNAY SAUCE

2 tablespoons butter
¼ cup flour
1¾ cups milk, scalded
½ teaspoon salt
  Dash of nutmeg
¼ cup cream
1 egg yolk
2 tablespoons grated Swiss cheese
2 tablespoons grated Parmesan cheese

1. Melt butter; blend in flour to make a roux. Add to scalded milk in double boiler, beating with a wire whisk until smooth and thick. Add salt and nutmeg.

2. Stir in cream and heat a few minutes longer. Add cheese and stir until melted.

3. Beat egg yolk, add some of the hot sauce, blend and return to double boiler stirring constantly. Remove from heat and serve.

# PEANUT BUTTER SAUCE

1 cup milk
1 tablespoon butter
2 tablespoons flour
½ teaspoon salt
2 tablespoons peanut butter

1. Scald milk.
2. Melt butter, blend in flour and salt; whip into milk. Cook, stirring, until it thickens.
3. Add peanut butter and stir until well blended. Delicious over broccoli.

## ZIPPY SAUCE

1 cup sour cream
2 tablespoons catsup
1 tablespoon lemon juice
1 tablespoon horseradish
1 teaspoon Worcestershire sauce
1 teaspoon curry powder
1 teaspoon dried dill weed
1 teaspoon dried parsley

Mix all ingredients and serve chilled.

*Note: This is good on cauliflower or broccoli.*

# TOMATO SAUCE FOR SPAGHETTI

⅔ cup chopped onion
1 clove garlic
2 tablespoons olive oil
3 cups stewed Italian tomatoes
1 cup tomato puree
½ teaspoon basil
½ teaspoon oregano
    Salt and pepper to taste

1. Sauté onion and garlic in oil for a few minutes in a heavy pot.

2. Put tomatoes through food mill or blend in blender. Add to onion mixture with tomato puree and seasonings.

3. Simmer to desired consistency.

*Note: You might like to add a few mushrooms.*

## VELVETY LEMON SAUCE

1½ tablespoons instant flour
¾ cup milk
½ teaspoon salt
Dash of MSG
¼ cup mayonnaise
1 tablespoon lemon juice

1. Dissolve flour in milk and stir until it thickens; add salt and MSG.

2. Add mayonnaise and lemon juice, stirring constantly.

3. A few drops of yellow food coloring may be added if desired.

# SWISS–DILL DIP

1 pound Swiss cheese
1½ large kosher dill pickles
1 cup mayonnaise

1. Grate cheese and pickles, or grind them if you prefer.
2. Add mayonnaise to cheese mixture.

*Note: This is also good on toasted rounds of bread or crisp crackers.*

# CHICK-PEA DIP

1 cup chick peas
3 tablespoons sesame oil
  Dash garlic powder
1½ tablespoons lemon juice
¼ teaspoon salt

Put all ingredients in the blender and blend until smooth.

# Eggs

"What monstrous folly ever led nature to create her one great enemy—man!"

Charles van Dyck

# CHINESE OMELET

½ cup raw rice
2 tablespoons butter or margarine
2 tablespoons flour
½ teaspoon salt
½ teaspoon dry mustard
½ cup milk, scalded in double boiler
1 cup grated sharp cheese
3 eggs, separated
¼ teaspoon MSG

1. Steam or boil rice; drain.

2. Melt butter; add flour, salt, dry mustard and MSG and blend. Whip into milk and cook until thick.

3. Add cheese, stir until melted. Add rice.

4. Beat egg yolks, add a little of the rice mixture, blend and return to double boiler and cook a few minutes longer, mixing well.

5. Beat egg whites until stiff but not dry. Fold into rice mixture.

6. Pour into a baking dish, buttered only on the bottom, and bake in a 325° oven until firm, about 40 minutes. Serve with tomato sauce.

# BAKED EGGS CREOLE

2 tablespoons chopped onion
2 tablespoons chopped green pepper
2 tablespoons chopped celery
2 tablespoons butter or margarine
1 tablespoon instant flour
2 cups stewed tomatoes, broken up
4 hard-cooked eggs, sliced
1 teaspoon sugar
  Salt and pepper
1 cup buttered bread crumbs

1. Sauté onion, pepper and celery in butter or margarine. Add flour; stir until smooth. Add tomatoes, stirring constantly. Cook until thick. Add sugar and salt and pepper to taste.

2. Put half the sauce in a buttered baking dish, arrange half the eggs over the sauce. Repeat.

3. Sprinkle buttered crumbs over the mixture. Bake in a 350° oven until heated through.

# SCRAMBLED EGGS WITH BEAN SPROUTS

2 tablespoons peanut oil
1 tablespoon minced onion
½ cup drained bean sprouts
2 eggs, slightly beaten
¼ teaspoon salt
1 teaspoon soy sauce
Dash of pepper

1. Sauté onions briefly in oil; add bean sprouts and mix.

2. Add soy sauce, salt and pepper to eggs and pour over the bean sprouts.

3. Cook over low heat, stirring frequently, until eggs are barely set but not hard.

# EASY BAKED MUSHROOM OMELET

4 eggs, separated
1 can condensed mushroom soup
2 tablespoons grated cheese

1. Beat egg whites until stiff but not dry.
2. Beat egg yolks until light and combine with soup.
3. Fold egg whites into soup mixture. Pour carefully into a 2-quart casserole which has been buttered on the bottom only. Sprinkle cheese on top.
4. Bake in a 350° oven about 30 minutes or until a knife inserted in the middle comes out clean.

# EGGS IN TOMATO CUPS

4 large firm tomatoes
4 eggs
   Salt, pepper, paprika
4 teaspoons butter
4 tablespoons seasoned bread crumbs

1. Cut a thin slice from stem end of tomatoes and remove part of the pulp, making space for the egg. Sprinkle with salt and pepper.
2. Break egg into tomato, sprinkle with more salt and pepper.
3. Sprinkle with seasoned bread crumbs; put one teaspoon butter on each and sprinkle with paprika.
4. Bake at 325° until eggs are done to your liking.
5. Serve plain or with mushroom or cheese sauce.

# DOUBLE ESCALLOPED ASPARAGUS AND EGGS

2 cups drained cooked asparagus, cut
    in pieces
1 can condensed cream of asparagus
    soup
4 hard-cooked eggs, sliced
1 cup cracker crumbs

1. Place half the asparagus in a buttered casserole. Put 2 of the eggs over it and pour half the soup over the eggs. Repeat.

2. Sprinkle cracker crumbs over soup and dot with butter. Bake in a 350° oven until brown and bubbly.

# EGG AND GREEN BEAN SCALLOP

2 tablespoons chopped pimiento
1 can condensed Cheddar cheese soup
6 hard-cooked eggs
2 cups cooked green beans, drained
1 cup bite-sized wheat cereal squares
2 tablespoons melted butter or
   margarine
½ teaspoon Worcestershire sauce

1. Add pimiento to soup.
2. Slice eggs and mix lightly with beans. Place in buttered baking dish. Pour sauce over beans and eggs, gently stirring to distribute sauce.
3. Combine cereal with melted butter or margarine and Worcestershire sauce. Sprinkle over top of casserole.
4. Bake about 25 minutes in a 350° oven until well heated through.

# NOODLES WITH DEVILED EGGS

4 ounces medium noodles
2 tablespoons butter
2 tablespoons flour
2 cups milk, scalded
½ teaspoon dry mustard
1 teaspoon salt
2 teaspoons instant onion flakes
½ teaspoon Worcestershire sauce
4 deviled eggs
¼ cup grated American cheese

1. Cook noodles until barely tender; drain, rinse with hot water and put in a buttered casserole.

2. Make a roux of butter, flour, mustard and salt and add to milk. Cook until thickened. Add onion flakes and Worcestershire sauce.

3. Make deviled eggs according to your favorite recipe. Place halves of eggs on top of noodles. Pour sauce over and sprinkle with cheese.

4. Bake in 350° oven until heated through—about 30 minutes.

# EGGS FLORENTINE

2 cups cooked spinach
4 eggs
1 cup grated sharp Cheddar cheese
   (4 ounces)
⅔ cup heavy cream
½ teaspoon Worcestershire sauce
⅔ cup buttered bread crumbs

1. Put ½ cup spinach in each of four individual casseroles, making a depression in the center. Break an egg into the depression and season with salt and pepper.

2. Heat cream and stir in cheese over low heat, stirring until cheese is melted. Add Worcestershire sauce.

3. Pour sauce over eggs. Top with buttered crumbs and bake in a 350° oven until eggs are set.

# Soups

"Men have heart attacks because they were born to be vegetarians but decided to eat meat."

Dr. Wm. S. Collens
Dr. Efstratios Vlahos
Gerald B. Dobkin
(World-Telegram—6/21/65)

# BEAN AND VEGETABLE SOUP

1 cup dried beans—lima, navy, or
   marrow
4 tablespoons margarine or butter
1 cup chopped onion
2 teaspoons salt
⅛ teaspoon pepper
1 bay leaf
2 cups canned or fresh tomatoes
2 carrots, diced
1 cup chopped celery

1. Wash beans; cover with water and soak overnight.

2. In the A.M., put beans in a large pot with one quart of water. Add onion, bay leaf, salt, pepper and butter or margarine. Add more water, if necessary, and boil slowly 1½ hours.

3. Add remaining vegetables and cook slowly until all vegetables are well done. Taste for seasoning. Remove bay leaf and serve.

# CHEESED VEGETABLE CHOWDER

1½ cups diced raw potatoes
½ cup chopped onion
¼ cup diced celery
1 teaspoon salt
¾ cup boiling water
2 cups heavy cream
¼ teaspoon dry mustard
  Dash of pepper
½ teaspoon Worcestershire sauce
¼ cup grated Cheddar cheese
1 cup tomatoes, broken up

1.  Simmer the potatoes, onion and celery in the boiling salted water about 15 minutes. Do not drain.

2.  Scald cream in double boiler.

3.  Add cheese to cream and stir until melted. Stir in the potato mixture.

4.  Add tomatoes slowly and the Worcestershire sauce, dry mustard and pepper. Heat but do not allow to curdle.

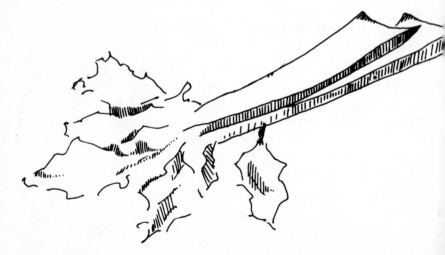

# CREAM SOUPS

If your budget or your figure won't allow heavy cream in your cream soups, resort to the following method:

1. Substitute an equal amount of milk for the cream specified in the recipe.

2. Scald the milk, reserving about half a cup.

3. For each cup of milk, dissolve 1 tablespoon instant flour in the reserved milk.

4. Whip flour mixture into scalded milk and cook until it thickens. Add a little butter or margarine, if you wish.

5. Add vegetable mixture to milk mixture and serve, seasoning to taste.

## CREAM OF CELERY SOUP

```
2 cups celery, cut in ½-inch pieces
2 tablespoons chopped onion
1½ cups boiling water
2 cups heavy cream
  Salt and pepper
  Dash of MSG
```

1. Cook celery and onion in boiling salted water until tender. Rub through a sieve, reserving liquid, or buzz in blender.

2. Add celery-onion mixture and liquid to scalded cream. Season with MSG, salt and pepper.

3. Pieces of raw celery, cut very fine, will add texture to the soup if added just before serving.

# CREAM OF SPINACH SOUP

1 cup cooked spinach
1 cup water or liquid from cooking
    spinach
1 teaspoon salt
2 cups heavy cream, scalded
    Dash of pepper and nutmeg

1. Put spinach through sieve or blender.
2. Add spinach and spinach water to cream and season to taste.

# CREAM OF MUSHROOM SOUP

½ pound fresh mushrooms
2 cups milk
1½ teaspoons salt
 Dash of pepper
 Dash of MSG
1 tablespoon butter
½ cup sour cream

1. Chop mushrooms coarsely and whirl in blender with some of the milk.

2. Heat blended mushrooms and remaining milk in double boiler. Add salt, pepper, MSG and butter.

3. When very hot, turn off heat and gradually beat in sour cream, beating until very smooth. Heat again, taking care that it doesn't curdle.

# CREAM OF TOMATO SOUP

  2 cups heavy cream
  1 bay leaf
  2 cups fresh stewed tomatoes, broken in
       small pieces
  1 teaspoon salt
    Pepper

1. Scald cream with bay leaf in a double boiler.
2. Heat tomatoes, add salt and add gradually to cream,
stirring constantly. Add a dash of pepper. Taste for seasoning. Remove bay leaf and serve.

# CREAM OF CORN SOUP

  2 cups cream-style corn
2½ cups heavy cream
  2 teaspoons instant onion flakes
  1 bay leaf
    Salt and pepper

1. Combine corn and cream.
2. Scald with bay leaf and onion flakes.
3. Remove bay leaf and season to taste with salt and pepper. Serve very hot.

## FARINA DUMPLINGS

    2 tablespoons butter
    1 cup milk
    ½ cup farina
    2 eggs, separated
    ½ teaspoon salt
      Dash of pepper
    ¼ teaspoon nutmeg
    ½ teaspoon dried parsley

1. Scald milk in double boiler with butter. Add farina gradually, stirring until thick. Cool.
2. Add egg yolks to farina mixture with nutmeg, salt, pepper and parsley. Fold in egg whites which have been stiffly beaten.
3. Drop very small amounts into boiling salted water and boil 10 minutes. They will triple in size.

# VERA'S NAVY BEAN SOUP

1 cup dried navy beans
5 cups cold water
1 cup chopped onion
1 cup chopped celery
1 cup chopped carrots
½ cup olive oil
1 cup tomato sauce
¼ cup chopped parsley
1 teaspoon MSG
Salt and pepper to taste

1. Wash beans. Soak overnight in cold water. In the morning, put on to boil.

2. Sauté onion, celery and carrots in olive oil, stirring frequently until golden.

3. Add sautéed vegetables and remaining ingredients to boiling beans. Simmer about 2 hours until beans are tender.

# VEGETABLE CHOWDER

2 teaspoons salt
Boiling water
2 cups diced raw potatoes
2 cups sliced or diced raw carrots
½ cup chopped onion
2 tablespoons butter
2 cups milk, scalded (use part cream,
if desired)
2 tablespoons flour
2 cups tomatoes
Salt and pepper

1. Cook potatoes and carrots until tender in boiling salted water to cover. Do not drain.

2. Sauté onion in butter until brown. Add flour and make a roux. Add to scalded milk, stirring constantly until thick.

3. Add tomatoes gradually to milk mixture, stirring constantly to avoid curdling. Add potatoes and carrots. Season to taste with salt and pepper.

# CORN CHOWDER

⅔ cup diced potatoes
2 tablespoons chopped onion
½ cup boiling water
3 cups milk, or part milk and part
    cream
    Half a bay leaf
1 cup whole-kernel corn
1½ teaspoons salt
    Dash of pepper
    Minced parsley

1. Boil the potatoes and onion in ½ cup boiling water until soft. Do not drain.

2. Scald the milk and cream with the bay leaf.

3. Add the cooked vegetables and the water in which they were cooked to the onion-potato mixture. Season with salt and pepper to taste. Remove bay leaf. Add parsley to garnish.

# VEGETABLE SOUP

⅓ cup chopped onion
1 tablespoon butter or margarine
¼ cup sliced carrots
¼ cup diced celery
2 tablespoons chopped parsley
Salt and pepper to taste
1 tablespoon uncooked barley
3 cups water
2 cups canned tomatoes
1 cup shredded cabbage
¼ cup green peas

1. Cook onion in butter or margarine until tender.
2. Add carrots, celery, parsley, salt, barley and water. Cook about 1 hour.
3. Add tomatoes and cabbage. Cook another ½ hour to blend flavors. Add more water, if needed.
4. Add peas and cook until tender.

# EASY TOMATO–CORN CHOWDER

1 cup cream-style corn
1 soup-can milk, scalded
1 can condensed tomato soup
½ teaspoon dried parsley flakes

1. Add corn to milk.
2. Add tomato soup to milk slowly, stirring constantly until very hot. Sprinkle with parsley and serve.

# Rice and Macaroni

"The way is hard: flesh is a habit that men enjoy as they enjoy drunkenness, dope and crime."

Tolstoy

# MACARONI LOAF

1 cup uncooked macaroni
2 cups milk, scalded
¼ cup butter or margarine
1⅓ cups soft bread crumbs
1 teaspoon salt
    Dash of pepper
¼ cup chopped pimientos
¼ cup chopped onion
¼ cup chopped celery
2 cups grated Cheddar cheese
4 eggs, slightly beaten

1. Cook macaroni according to package directions, drain.

2. Combine remaining ingredients. Add macaroni and mix gently.

3. Pour into greased loaf pan. Bake at 325° about 45 minutes or until a knife inserted in the middle comes out clean. Let stand 10 minutes.

4. Invert on serving platter. Serve with tomato sauce.

# BAKED RICE

2 eggs, slightly beaten
1 cup milk, scalded
Few gratings nutmeg
1 teaspoon salt
2 teaspoons brown sugar
1 teaspoon instant onion flakes
1⅓ cups cooked rice

1. Add scalded milk to eggs gradually; add seasonings and onion flakes.

2. Add rice and pour into a buttered baking dish. Set in a pan of hot water and bake about 30 minutes in a 350° oven or until a knife inserted in the middle comes out clean.

## NOODLES, GERMAN STYLE

¼ pound medium noodles
1 can condensed cream of celery soup
½ cup grated Swiss cheese
½ teaspoon salt
¼ teaspoon paprika
Dash of pepper
3 eggs, slightly beaten

1. Cook the noodles; drain and rinse.
2. Heat the soup in a double boiler; add cheese, salt, pepper and paprika, stirring until the cheese melts.
3. Add the soup mixture to the noodles. Add the eggs.
4. Pour into a greased baking pan and bake in a 375° oven until a knife inserted in the middle comes out clean. Cut in squares to serve.

# MACARONI SPECIAL

  1 cup elbow macaroni, uncooked
  ½ cup soft bread crumbs
  ¼ cup melted butter
  2 tablespoons chopped pimientos
  2 tablespoons chopped green pepper
  2 teaspoons grated onion
  1 cup grated Cheddar cheese
1½ teaspoons salt
1½ cups milk, scalded
  3 eggs, separated

1. Cook macaroni in salted water until tender. Drain.
2. Combine bread crumbs, butter, pimientos, peppers, onion, salt and cheese. Add milk.
3. Pour over egg yolks, mixing well. Add macaroni.
4. Beat egg whites until stiff but not dry and fold into macaroni mixture.
5. Pour into buttered casserole, set in a pan of hot water and bake 40–50 minutes, until firm, in a 350° oven.

# TOMATO LUNCHEON CASSEROLE

½ cup raw rice
½ cup elbow macaroni or ditalini
3 medium potatoes, diced
3 tablespoons butter or margarine
3 cups stewed tomatoes
2 teaspoons salt
½ teaspoon pepper

1. Cook rice for 10 minutes in boiling salted water. Add macaroni and cook 5 minutes longer. Add potatoes and cook until tender. Drain well.

2. Sauté onions in butter or margarine until golden brown. Add to rice mixture. Add tomatoes, salt and pepper.

3. Put in buttered baking dish and heat in 375° oven until bubbling.

# SPICY GOLDEN RICE

4 tablespoons peanut oil
2 bay leaves
1 teaspoon salt
1 2-inch piece stick cinnamon
2 pounded cardamom seeds
½ teaspoon tumeric
⅛ teaspoon powdered saffron
1½ cups boiling water
1½ cups instant rice

1. Add oil and seasonings to water. Let stand 15 minutes.

2. Bring water to a boil again, add rice and let stand 5 minutes.

3. Remove cinnamon and bay leaves and serve.

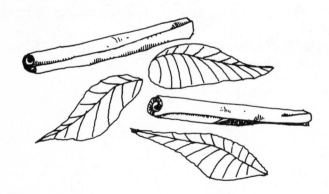

## TIBETAN RICE

1 cup raw rice
3 tablespoons peanut oil
2 cups boiling water
½ teaspoon tumeric
½ teaspoon curry powder
1 teaspoon salt
6 tablespoons currants or raisins

1. In a heavy skillet, mix the rice with the peanut oil and brown slightly. Add boiling water, raisins or currants and spices. Cover.

2. Cook slowly, adding a little more water, if necessary, until each grain of rice is separate and tender. Avoid overcooking or it will become soggy.

# INDIAN RICE AND PEAS

4 tablespoons peanut oil
2 bay leaves
1 2-inch stick cinnamon
4 pounded cardamom seeds
1 teaspoon cumin
1 teaspoon salt
2 tablespoons instant onion
1½ cups boiling water
1½ cups instant rice
½ cup cooked peas

1. Add oil and seasonings to water. Let stand 15 minutes.

2. Bring to boil again and add rice. Let stand 5 minutes.

3. Remove cinnamon and bay leaves and mix peas in gently.

# INA'S MANDARIN RICE

1 1-pound can mandarin oranges
1 cup raw rice
½ cup currants
½ cup onion, chopped
¼ cup margarine
½ cup toasted slivered almonds
2 tablespoons frozen orange juice
   concentrate

1. Drain mandarin oranges, reserving juice.
2. Add mandarin juice to salted boiling water and cook rice until tender. Drain.
3. Sauté onion in margarine until brown. Add currants, almonds, mandarins and orange concentrate and heat. Fold into rice. Serve hot.

# RICE–CHEESE CASSEROLE

2 cups cooked rice
1 cup shredded sharp Cheddar cheese
1 can condensed tomato soup
½ teaspoon salt
Dash of pepper
¼ teaspoon dry mustard
½ teaspoon Worcestershire sauce
2 eggs, slightly beaten
2 teaspoons instant onion flakes

1. Combine all ingredients.
2. Pour into a greased baking dish. Bake about 45 minutes or until firm in a 350° oven.

# LENTILS AND RICE

1 cup lentils
1 cup raw rice
4 tablespoons butter or margarine
2 medium onions, chopped
Salt and pepper to taste

1. Cook lentils and rice separately in boiling salted water. Drain well.
2. Sauté onions in butter until brown. Add to rice and mix well. Add lentils and taste for seasoning.
3. Place in casserole and heat through.

# Miscellaneous

"We have dined and whereas the slaughter house is gracefully hidden by a multitude of miles, there is complicity."

Emerson

# CRÊPES

2 eggs, well beaten
⅔ cup flour, sifted twice before measuring
1½ tablespoons sugar
½ teaspoon salt
1 cup milk

1. Combine all ingredients and beat until very smooth. A blender does it perfectly.

2. Melt a teaspoon of butter in a heavy 6-inch skillet. Pour in a small amount of batter, tilting pan to spread batter, and fry until light brown. Turn and barely cook other side.

3. Stack on a platter until ready to use.

*Note: Although this is the recipe my friends follow, I prefer to add a generous amount of melted butter or vegetable oil—as much as ¼ cup—right to the batter. If you put in shortening while batter is thick, it won't separate even when your batter is thinned and you won't have to grease the skillet.*

# ESCALLOPED APPLES

4 cups peeled, diced cooking apples
2 cups bread crumbs
¼ cup melted butter or margarine
¼ cup brown sugar
　Dash of salt
　Few gratings nutmeg
2 teaspoons lemon juice
½ cup hot water or fruit juice

1. Combine bread crumbs with butter or margarine, brown sugar, salt and nutmeg.

2. Put half the crumb mixture in shallow buttered baking dish, add apples and remaining crumbs.

3. Mix lemon juice and water and pour over. Bake in 350° oven until crumbs are brown and apples are tender. Time will depend on how firm the apples are.

# GNOCCHI

2 cups milk
½ cup farina
1 teaspoon salt
4 tablespoons grated Parmesan cheese
1 egg, beaten
Flour
Bread crumbs

1. Scald milk, add farina slowly, stirring constantly to avoid lumps. Add salt and cheese and cook until thick.

2. Pour onto wet 8 x 8-inch shallow pan, smoothing the top. Chill.

3. Cut in squares; dip in flour, egg and crumbs.

4. Place on greased platter and bake in a 400° oven until brown, or sauté in butter on both sides.

5. Serve with tomato sauce or catsup.

# EUNICE'S GREEN TOMATO MINCEMEAT

3 pounds green tomatoes
3 pounds cooking apples
2 pounds raisins
3 pounds light brown sugar
2 tablespoons salt
1 cup butter or margarine
1 cup cider vinegar
2 tablespoons cinnamon
2 teaspoons cloves
1 teaspoon nutmeg

1. Grind tomatoes with medium blade of food chopper. Drain and measure juice. Add an equal amount of water.

2. Scald tomatoes and drain. Repeat twice the process of adding fresh water, scalding and draining.

3. Peel apples and grind. Grind raisins; add apples and raisins to tomatoes with sugar, salt and butter or margarine and cook until clear.

4. Add vinegar and spices. Cook until thick.

5. Pack into hot sterilized jars and seal.

# THERESA'S RIBBON VEGETABLE LOAF

Green pepper rings
Carrots cut lengthwise in ¼-inch strips
Young green beans
Butternut squash
Salt and pepper

1. Cover the bottom of a loaf pan with pepper rings. Sprinkle with salt and pepper.

2. Place carrot strips lengthwise of the pan, over pepper rings. Sprinkle with salt and pepper.

3. Place green beans crosswise of the pan over the carrots, cutting to fit the pan. Sprinkle with salt and pepper.

4. Cut slices of squash ½-inch thick (cut from the stem end to get solid slices) and place over green beans, trimming to fit pan. Sprinkle with salt and pepper. Dot with butter and pour about 2 tablespoons of water in pan.

5. Cover with aluminum foil and bake in a 350° oven about 45 minutes until vegetables are tender. Turn upside down on a platter to serve.

# SPANISH FONDUE

6 tablespoons chopped onion
4 tablespoons chopped green pepper
2 tablespoons butter
⅔ cup whole-kernel corn
⅔ cup canned or fresh tomatoes,
    drained
1 cup milk, scalded
1⅓ cups soft bread crumbs
1 cup grated sharp cheese
½ teaspoon Worcestershire sauce
1 teaspoon salt
  Dash of pepper
2 eggs, slightly beaten

1. Sauté onion and peppers in butter for five minutes. Add the corn and tomatoes. Lightly sprinkle with salt and pepper and turn into a buttered casserole.

2. Add bread crumbs to milk. Let stand a few minutes and add cheese, Worcestershire sauce, salt and pepper. Add eggs, mix well and pour carefully over vegetable mixture.

3. Bake in a 350° oven until a knife inserted in the cheese mixture comes out clean—about 30 minutes. Serve upside down. Corn may be omitted.

# M. J.'S PEANUT LOAF

2½ cups stale bread, cubed
1 cup milk, scalded
½ teaspoon salt
½ teaspoon MSG
3 tablespoons peanut butter
2 eggs
1 teaspoon instant onion flakes
1 cup diced celery
1 cup peanuts, ground

1. Add bread to milk and let stand until milk is absorbed.

2. Add salt, MSG, peanut butter, eggs and instant onion and mix well.

3. Add celery and peanuts.

4. Pour into greased loaf pan and bake 45 minutes in a 350° oven or until firm in the middle.

*Note: May be served with celery sauce or peanut butter sauce.*

# HAZEL'S VEGETABLE STUFFING

3 tablespoons butter or margarine
2 carrots, shredded
2 stalks celery, diced fine
1 small onion, minced
½ cup water
1 teaspoon dried parsley
¼ teaspoon thyme
¼ teaspoon savory
4 slices cracked wheat bread, diced

1. Melt butter or margarine in a heavy pan. Add carrots, celery, onion. Sauté a few minutes. Add water. Cover and steam 5 minutes.
2. Remove cover, add herbs and bread.

*Note: This makes a good stuffing for acorn squash.*

# VEGETABLE PIE

2 tablespoons chopped onion
2 tablespoons butter
1 tablespoon flour
1½ teaspoons salt
⅛ teaspoon pepper
2 cups cooked mixed vegetables
1 egg, slightly beaten
1 cup mashed potatoes, well seasoned
Paprika
2 tablespoons grated Parmesan cheese

1. Sauté onion in butter until golden. Add flour, salt and pepper, blending well.

2. Add undrained vegetables and simmer until the mixture thickens, stirring constantly. Pour into greased casserole.

3. Beat egg and potatoes until light. Spread over vegetable mixture, using a pastry tube if desired. Sprinkle with cheese and paprika.

4. Bake in a 375° oven until brown.

# SQUASH MUFFINS

¾ cup cooked mashed winter squash
½ cup milk
1 egg, well beaten
4 tablespoons melted butter or
    margarine
1½ cups flour
½ teaspoon salt
⅓ cup sugar
1 tablespoon baking powder


1. Combine squash with milk, egg and melted butter or margarine.

2. Mix and sift together the dry ingredients.

3. Add the liquids to the flour mixture and barely mix.

4. Put in greased muffin pan. Bake 20 minutes at 400°. Makes 12.

## OPEN APPLE–CHEESE SANDWICH

1 split English muffin
Mayonnaise
Slices of eating apple to cover—
 Cortlands or McIntosh are good
2 1-ounce slices of American cheese

1. Spread muffin with mayonnaise. Put slices of peeled apple to cover muffin, then cover with a slice of cheese.
2. Broil until cheese melts and browns. Serves 1.

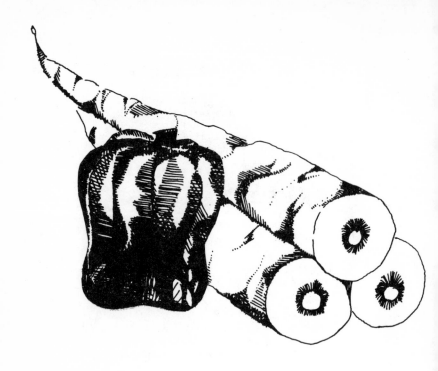

## RAW CARROT RELISH

1 cup ground carrot
¼ cup ground green pepper
½ cup finely chopped celery
¼ cup minced onion
½ teaspoon salt
2 tablespoons vinegar
2 tablespoons honey

Combine all ingredients. Let stand a while to season.

# VEGETABLE FRITTERS

1¾ cups sifted flour
1 teaspoon salt
Dash of pepper
1 tablespoon baking powder
2 eggs, well beaten
½ cup milk
2 tablespoons cooking oil
1 cup cooked mixed vegetables, drained
1 tablespoon finely chopped parsley

1. Mix and sift dry ingredients.
2. Combine eggs, milk and oil and add all at once to dry ingredients and beat well. Add vegetables and parsley.
3. Drop by tablespoons into hot fat, 375°, and fry until a delicate brown. Drain on paper towels.
4. Serve with cheese sauce.

"He that killeth an ox is as if he slew a man."

Book of Isaiah

# Desserts

"For lions and tigers slaughter is the only means of sustenance, whereas to you it is superfluous luxury and crime."

Pythagoras

# APPLE FRITTERS

1 egg, well beaten
½ cup milk
1 cup sifted flour
2 teaspoons baking powder
¼ teaspoon salt
½ teaspoon cinnamon
2 tablespoons sugar
2 apples, peeled and cut in thin slices

1. Combine egg and milk.
2. Mix and sift together the dry ingredients. Add to milk mixture and blend. Add apples.
3. Fry in deep hot fat, 375°, dropping by spoonfuls.
4. Serve hot with maple syrup or dust with confectioners' sugar.

# BAKED GRAPEFRUIT #1

*For each grapefruit half:*

> 1 tablespoon maple syrup
> 1 teaspoon butter

1. Cut out center core of grapefruit and loosen segments.
2. Pour syrup over and dot with butter.
3. Bake in 375° oven about 10 minutes or broil until brown.

# BAKED GRAPEFRUIT #2

*For each grapefruit half:*

> 1 tablespoon light brown sugar
> Dash of cinnamon
> 1 teaspoon butter

Combine sugar and cinnamon and prepare as for Baked Grapefruit #1.

## CHOCOLATE CHIP BREAD PUDDING

2 cups soft bread cubes
½ cup semi-sweet chocolate bits
2 eggs, slightly beaten
½ cup sugar
Dash of salt
1½ cups milk, scalded
½ teaspoon vanilla

1. Place bread cubes in a baking dish. Sprinkle chocolate chips over bread.

2. Mix sugar, salt and eggs. Add milk and vanilla and pour over bread.

3. Place baking dish in a pan of hot water and bake at 350°, until a knife inserted in the middle comes out clean.

# COCONUT PEACH SHORTCAKE

2 cups sifted flour
1 tablespoon baking powder
½ teaspoon salt
2 tablespoons sugar
¼ cup fine coconut
¼ cup vegetable shortening
⅔ cup milk
1 quart sliced peaches, sweetened
   to taste

1. Mix and sift dry ingredients. Add coconut. Cut in shortening until fine. Add milk all at once.

2. Spread dough into greased 9-inch layer pan. Bake about 20 minutes in a 400° oven.

3. Split, butter layers if desired. Put half the peaches on bottom layer, place other half on top and spread remaining peaches over it.

4. Garnish with whipped cream and coconut.

*Note: Use 2 cups prepared biscuit mix if you wish, adding the sugar and coconut.*

# DEEP DISH PIES

1. Fill individual casseroles with fruit sweetened to taste.

2. Make your favorite pastry using sherry instead of water.

3. Wet rims of casseroles and cover tops with pastry. Cut vents in pastry.

4. Brush tops with cream and bake at 375° until fruit is done.

# GREEN GRAPES WITH SOUR CREAM

*For each serving:*

    ½ cup green grapes
    2 tablespoons sour cream
    1 tablespoon maple syrup

1. If the grapes are not seedless, split and remove seeds.

2. Put grapes in serving dish, spread sour cream over, then drizzle the maple syrup over the cream.

# GLAZED APPLES

6 baking apples
½ cup sugar
¼ cup white corn syrup
1 cup water
3 slices lemon
1 cardamom seed
¼ cup sugar
2 tablespoons honey

1. Core apples and pare ⅓ of the way down.
2. Combine ½ cup sugar and corn syrup with water. Add lemon slices and the kernels from the cardamom seed. Bring to a boil in electric skillet set at 225°.
3. Place apples upside down in syrup and cook, covered, until soft but not mushy. Turn right side up and continue cooking until done.
4. Remove apples to a flat pan. Pour syrup over them. Sprinkle a teaspoon of sugar over each apple. Put under broiler until sugar melts. Baste with syrup. Repeat.
5. Drizzle a teaspoon of honey over each apple. Broil until glazed. Chill and serve cold.

*Note: Cortland apples are not primarily considered a baking apple, but are very good in this recipe. If you want a pretty pink syrup, cook the peel from the top in the syrup while simmering the apples. Remove before glazing. Or, do it the easy way—add a few drops of red food color.*

# LEMON ICE CREAM

1 pint vanilla ice cream
6 tablespoons frozen lemonade
concentrate

1. Soften ice cream and stir in lemonade concentrate.
2. Put in ice tray and freeze until firm.

# OLGA'S OATMEAL–APPLESAUCE PUDDING

1 cup flour
1 cup quick-cooking oatmeal
½ teaspoon baking soda
½ teaspoon salt
½ cup light brown sugar
½ teaspoon cinnamon
½ cup butter or margarine
2 cups applesauce

1. Combine flour, oatmeal, soda, salt, sugar and cinnamon. Cut in butter or margarine until coarse crumbs are formed.
2. Put half the mixture in an 8 x 8-inch pan. Spread applesauce over crumbs, sprinkle remaining crumbs on top.
3. Bake in a 375° oven about 40 minutes, until crumbs are brown and crusty. Cut in squares.

# PUMPKIN COOKIES

1 cup vegetable shortening
1 cup plus 2 tablespoons sugar
1 cup cooked mashed pumpkin
½ teaspoon vanilla extract
2 cups flour
1 teaspoon salt
1 teaspoon cinnamon
¼ teaspoon nutmeg
½ teaspoon ginger
3 teaspoons baking powder
¾ cup raisins
½ cup nuts, chopped

1. Cream shortening; add sugar and blend well. Add pumpkin and vanilla and mix well.
2. Mix and sift dry ingredients. Add to creamed mixture.
3. Add raisins and nuts.
4. Drop by a teaspoon onto a greased cookie sheet. Bake at 400° 8–10 minutes.

# RHUBARB PUDDING

*Batter*

> 1 cup sifted flour
> ½ cup sugar
> 2 teaspoons baking powder
> ½ teaspoon salt
> ¼ cup butter or margarine
> ½ cup milk

*Topping*

> 2 cups rhubarb, cut in ½-inch pieces
> 1 cup sugar
> 1 cup boiling water

1. Mix and sift dry ingredients. Cut in butter or margarine until fine. Add milk all at once and mix. Spread batter in an 8 x 8-inch pan.

2. Arrange rhubarb over batter. Melt the sugar in the boiling water and pour over all.

3. Bake 45 minutes in a 375° oven.

# POACHED PEARS

        4 pears
    1½ cups water
    ½ cup sugar
    ¼ cup white corn syrup
        4 slices lemon
        2 tablespoons chopped crystallized
            ginger

1. Peel, halve and core pears.
2. Combine remaining ingredients and bring to a boil in a large saucepan. Add pears. Simmer until tender. Serve chilled.

# INDEX

## C